LOVE
MECHANICS

Power Tools To Build Successful Relationships With Women

Volume I

Renee Piane

www.LoveMechanics.com

WHAT OTHERS ARE SAYING ABOUT LOVE MECHANICS

"Renee has crafted a user-friendly roadmap to guide men as they traverse some fairly complex relationship terrain. My recommendation to single men is: Don't leave home without your copy of *Love Mechanics*."
--Stephen Johnson, Ph.D., Psychotherapist and Director of The Men's Center of Los Angeles, Ca.

"This book is an invaluable resource providing practical tools for any man who is looking for a casual relationship or seeking their soul mate."
--Linda Stick, M.A, Founder of The Center for Shyness

"Renee hands you a toolbox full of witty, clever and inspiring relationship tools that make 'getting under the hood' of your relationship fun and easy!"
--Lynelle Goodreau, MFCC

"The skill sharpening tools in 'Love Mechanics' will educate men to balance all areas of their lives. The life changing results will build confidence and power - qualities most women look for in a man."
--William Cole Smith, C.E.O. Digital Education

"As a fitness expert who works with the mind/body connection, I have to say Renee Piane's book "Love Mechanics" really hits home. Renee and I have always agreed that in order to realize long-term outer change, inner change has to occur first. I think everyone who wants to improve their love life should read *Love Mechanics.*"
--Michael George, Fitness Expert

"Many men are confused and clueless. If you're looking for the secrets of women...listen carefully to Renee Piane. She has a unique way of teaching men the dynamics of the dating game. Renee knows more about what singles really need than anyone in the field. Thank you, Renee."
--Michael Edwards, MFCC

ABOUT THE AUTHOR

Renee Piane

The author of "Love Mechanics," Renee Piane, is a widely acclaimed and sought-after inspirational speaker and dating consultant whose life's work is devoted to educating men and women about how to become fulfilled in their own lives, develop lasting relationships and find true love.

In demand as a personal empowerment coach, image consultant and communications expert, Renee draws from her fifteen years of research in psychology, sociology and the healing arts. She is certified in NLP (Neuro Linguistic Programming), time-line therapy and hypnotherapy.

Renee was inspired to write "Love Mechanics" after conducting hundreds of in-depth interviews with single men across the U.S. for the cable special, "Men Across America." She has also interviewed countless relationship experts, doctors and authors on the topics of love, sex, healthy living and energy research and was hard-pressed to find any credible resources offering these vital guidelines for single people.

This discovery compelled her to research and compile her own material that would more completely address man's universal need for acceptance and love in the 21st Century. "Love Mechanics" is the first in a series of books that Renee Piane is currently writing.

Her online radio show, "Love Mechanics" has just debuted on Success Talk Radio to provide weekly tips, inspiring messages and interviews with experts (www.Success-Talk.com/piane.htm).

Renee has hosted and been featured on more than 25 different TV shows including The "X" Show (FX), "Love Chronicles" (A&E), "New Attitudes" (Lifetime), "The Debra Duncan Show" (ABC), "A.M. Philadelphia," the TV special, "How A Gentleman Should Treat A Lady" (Lifetime), and "Men Are From Mars, Women are from Venus" (nationally syndicated)

She writes a weekly column for Entertainment Today entitled, "SingleZone" and has been featured in Los Angeles Times, Cosmopolitan among many others.

Born and raised in Wilmington, Delaware, Renee was inspired at a young age by the philanthropic works of her father, who created programs to feed the homeless and house the aged and her mother Angela, whose door is always open to counsel and heal friends and family with her loving nature.

Renee formed her company, LOVEWORKS, in 1995 with the goal of becoming a catalyst for affecting positive change in people's interpersonal lives, thus building stronger communities. Her popular networking events in Los Angeles and her own dedication to helping non-profit organizations has encouraged many single people to volunteer their time and efforts to help raise funds for worthy causes.

Using her abundant charm, charisma and infectious optimism, Renee teaches that by *"Flirting With Life"* and giving back, we all can attain more success in life and love than they ever dreamed possible!

This Book is Dedicated to ...

My parents Angela and Robert Piane who have truly lived lives of unconditional love and committment in good times and in hardship.

Their love and devotion to our family and their never ending service to the world has been weaved into the fabric of my soul.

I love you for always being there for me. I am blessed to have you for my parents. Love Works!

ACKNOWLEDGEMENTS

What an adventure it is to write a book. Amazing how a hobby turned into a life mission. With the loving support, encouragement and guidance of friends, family, clients and business people from all walks of my life this dream has become a reality.

Drew (Big Daddy) Clausen has supported me every step of the way and I am eternally grateful that he believed in me. He has provided me with the opportunity to publish and market this book and share his dog Chuck "the Madman" with me. Chuck has provided me with love, kisses and companionship during many long nights of writing.

The very first inspiration for this was Peter Johnson who asked me to teach a men's seminar with him over 7 years ago and Andrew Maltin who convinced me that writing a book was the way to market myself.

After being mentored by Susan Levine (Speakersservices.com) and Sylvia Newton Robbins (formally from The American Seminars Leaders Training), I was given the directions to begin this project. With the support of friends (Sylvia, Dr. Nina Craft, Ruth Bergeson, Scott Viers, Juliann Pederson, Cheryl Kugel, Gregory Forrest, Dr. Don, Paul Cunningham) the mechanics theme was created and the work began.

Karen Minutelli (alias Hawk Eye) was the first person to make this book real for me by diligently transcribing my seminars and making sense of my notes written in journals. She actually created the first version of the book as I continued my writing. Karen, thank you for working many long nights to build the foundation for my dream. With the talents of Jack Barnard, Peter Riekhart, Scott Foster and Herb Friedman (a great friend who meticulously organized and corrected the final version of the book) and finally the artistic talents, editing and internal design of Tony Kogak, this book finally got completed. We spent many an hour pasting and clicking with many laughs in between.

Bart Smith, TheMarketingMan.com, has truly added magic to my personal marketing plan and to the creation of the eBook version of "Love Mechanics." Bart motivated me beyond my limits!

There are so many people that contributed their time and talents for this to have manifested. Brett Taylor (my brother-in-law) who created the first design of the book cover (along with Rush Rhoades). Brett supported me and added to my business plan (along with Gregory Forrest and Herb Friedman) which has brought my whole life to a new level. These dedicated friends added the professional touches that created a winning formula for my business.

The book cover was then turned over to Jason Arthur, a creative graphic artist, whose patience and artistic talents will be honored since I drove him crazy with changes. Then finally, the project was completed by Mark Hogan from Digital Education. Thanks to all of you!

I must also thank Cole Smith, President of Digital Education Corporation and his "power team," Angela, Mark, Gary, Matthew and Barbara, who helped me during the development phases of *Love Mechanics*.

To all of my friends who contributed their support and energy by listening and supporting me such as: Drew, Herb (all those hours fixing my computer and setting up my home with your tool box), Clark (your humor, hugs and words of wisdom), Scott Foster (all your healing energy and support), Ruthie (all those seminars you assisted, typing and events you volunteered to do), Rhonda, Lynette, Susan, Dr. Michele McMillian, Kim Rahilly (fabulous PR), Lizzy and Raul, Suzanne (my NLP buddy), Lynda G, Esti, Karen D, Jayne Major, Joe Reber, Isabel Kleigman (your inspiration) and all of my devoted clients. Richard Hatch (my former radio show partner), Katherine Alice (prayers and contribution of great ideas), Scott Viers and Lucien Lacasse (who both help me with my client's homes and creating my environment at work and at home). Dr. Toby Watkinson (the best doctor, teacher and friend), Katheline Mac Namara (years of prayer), Michael Pederson and Bob Rami (who both give me awesome body work and energy tune-ups), Joe Paolillo (my friend and loyal assistant) and The Good News Network Team: Paige, Donnie, Steve and Todd (they taught me what commitment is).

I must acknowledge my friends Paul Stienbaum, Sean Salas, Michael Edwards, Gerald Saldo, Larry, and Randy (all dedicated friends who helped produce, edit and support me through all my Love Works TV shows and demo reels).

More thanks goes to: Randy Catanese and Esti Miller (great legal advice), JJ, Bo Tomlin, Chuck Hirsch (my first hypnotherapist), Terry Braverman and John Salazar (owner of Entertainment Today where my column runs weekly). My Mastermind group: Paula, Heidi, Nan, Susan, Sylvia, and JQ. My co-workers and special friends: Sherri Smith (my angel sister that owns the dating service Elite Connections and has helped me through many rough times), Kerri Roberts and Gerri Blender.

To my teachers and mentors: my parents, Robert and Angela Piane and all of my brothers and sisters: Theresa, Bob Jr., Bryan, Joesph, Angel and extended family (my niece and nephews, aunts, uncles, cousins...) I love them all!

Other great mentors and inspirations for me are Dr. Reverand Michael Beckwith, Gary De Rodriquez, Jeffrey Armstrong, Louise Hay, Dr. Wayne Dyer, Mark Victor Hansen, Leo Buscalia, Nathaniel Brandon, Anthony Robbins, Barbara DeAngeles, Les Brown, Norman Vincent Peale, Rumi, Dan Pointer, Joel Roberts, Sylvia Newton Robbins and Susan Levin.

I also want to thank all the men and women who have come to hear me speak, attended my networking events and taken my seminars. You are all my teachers. The encouragement, support and inspiration kept me going when I sometimes wanted to give up on completing this book. Believe me, I have been privileged to experience each and every session and I have grown from working with each person that has crossed my path. I am most grateful to GOD who has truly blessed me with this opportunity to share my work and passion with you right now. I have changed while writing this book and this experience is life expanding.

I must also thank all the men I have loved in my life, who have contributed to the making of this book. You know who you are and you will always have a place in my heart! Each relationship has contributed to the growth of my heart and soul. Thanks for the lessons on love!

LOVE

MECHANICS

The Power Tools To Build Successful Relationships With Women

Volume I

Renee Piane

Love Mechanics

"Power Tools To Build Successful Relationships with Women"
by Renee Piane

For more information about LOVE MECHANICS, please contact us at our website (www.LoveMechanics.com) or the address or phone number below. To order more copies use the order form in the back of the book or give us a call for information about distribution and wholesale prices.

Interested distributors contact:

The Claus Group
13078 Mindanao Way
Suite 314
Marina Del Ray, CA 90292
Office (310) 827-7882
Email: Drewclaus@aol.com

© Copyright January, 2000. All Rights Reserved.
Printed in the United States of America.

ISBN # 0-9678964-0-1

Library of Congress Cataloging-in–Publication Data
Piane, Renee
Love Mechanics "Power Tools To Build Successful Relationships with Women"
Self help/motivation/relationships

Photography by Carl Studna
Book layout and design by Anthony Kogak
Book cover design by Mark Hogan & Jason Arthur

Table of Contents

PART TWO
THE EXTERNAL TUNE-UP

PART THREE
ON THE ROAD TO SUCCESS

INTRODUCTION

I'm so pleased and honored that you are reading this book. It shows that you are interested in building successful connections with women and investigating the effective tools available to win in the game of love!

I bravely and lovingly present the female perspective and a process that has worked for thousands of men. Many men are confused about how to deal with the new women out there who are self-sufficient, powerful and independent. In the privacy of your home, *Love Mechanics* will instill you with confidence and offer you easy tools to get instant results with women!

We all need tune-ups for our cars — what about our love lives? Do you even have a love life or want one? Or have you given up on creating love in your life? Are you still single or newly single again and feel confused? Are you frustrated or unfulfilled with your current relationship, but afraid to be alone? Maybe you just have a "dead engine" on the whole subject?

Well, how about a tune-up? An overhaul? Or at least a good look under the hood? To get where you want to go, you need to keep your car in magnificent running order. Can't the same be said for you?

Have no fear, *Love Mechanics* will get you back on the road with power tools of self-awareness, energy and connection. You will learn vital information that will change your relationships in all areas of your life — especially with women!

Here in the 21st Century, singles are making brave new choices. To make these choices, they need to check out all the options, tools and mechanics of connecting in these busy times and creating a foundation for good relationships.

This book is designed to offer simple guidelines to assist us all to first develop the qualities in ourselves that we are looking for in others, then to connect in long-term relationships or decide that long-term isn't what we want for our lives. The divorce rate is almost 65% nationwide! I used to ask myself "what can I do in life that can contribute to love and what would make a difference?" This book is one of those contributions!

There is a huge need for education to teach singles to be fulfilled in spite of being alone so they don't marry for the wrong reasons and end up disappointed and divorced. Many have to learn these lessons later in life and unfortunately pass the sadness onto the children of their broken relationships. I suppose that pain and growth is a part of the life process and if my words can assist in creating healthier foundations for self- love and relationships, then I have lived my vision. I only wish I had learned this information when I was in my teens to save myself from going through all the growing pains it took to learn these lessons.

Let's face it, we didn't learn very much about love, relationships and the opposite sex from our parents. Many people were brought up in single parent homes and didn't receive any guidance at all. The statistics today show that even with both parents at home, the average time spent alone with a child or teen is about 10 minutes a day. Unfortunately, discussing intimate topics usually isn't covered in that short amount of time. Too many parents believe you will learn all you need to know about sex and dating in school or on television. What a joke!

Who taught you? Who were your role models for relationships? Where did you get guidance? Your dad? Your mother? Your algebra teacher? Your coach? Your friends?

I've interviewed hundreds of men about this topic. Many expressed that no one taught them love skills. They learned by observing. *"Observing whom?"* I asked. *"Your jock buddies? Playboy? Penthouse? Hustler?"* Not a great source of illumination. The fact is, 90 percent of the women in the world don't look like the women in those magazines, so many of you are fantasizing about the unattainable woman. No wonder you're not getting the results you desire and believe you never will.

Think of how much time you spend learning to master a sport or to successfully play the stock market. Now compare that with how little time you spend learning how to create a healthy relationship and to discover what you really want out of life. I must be honest with you: most men know way too little about the mysteries of women and love, and yet the decision we make when choosing a mate is one of the most important decisions of our life! Men and women are brought up to believe vastly different things about love and romance, yet men are supposed to know intuitively how to love women and be suddenly prepared for marriage and commitment? Women believe that men know what we expect them to say and do, and we get disappointed that you aren't following the "rules" we have lived by for so long. I know now that these supposed "rules" and expectations need to be understood by men so that we will all be communicating more effectively and not get repeatedly disappointed in the game of love.

Connecting with women these days can be difficult for some men. Women are trained from birth to find their "prince" and to help and guide each other, but men mostly "roll with the punches," unless they have been fortunate enough to be graced with great female friends or strong family role models.

Generally speaking, women read books and go to support groups when they want guidance. In fact, women are almost "drowning" in information to find "Mr. Right"! Here are just a few examples of the books that curious women read: *Embracing the Beloved; Men are From Mars, Women are from Venus; The Rules;* and *Getting to I Do.* Women attempt to unravel the mystery. On the other side of the relationship coin, many men do search for information, but too often they don't want other men to know about it. They're afraid it makes them look like losers and yet many men are hungering to learn more. Now men everywhere are reaching out for information, and we are so glad you are taking action! You will now be in charge of creating yourself from the inside out.

To the Rescue...*Love Mechanics* will give your love life a lift and assist you in creating a fulfilling life whether you have a significant other or not. There will be no man-bashing, just honesty and wisdom that comes from many years of experience in this field. You might say that I have been engaged in the ultimate "Prince" training. Many men claim not to want any direction in this area, yet the men who have read advance copies of *Love Mechanics* say that they wish they'd had a book like this when they were younger to help them through so many confidence issues and challenges with women.

I began consulting singles regarding their private dating challenges and I prepared them for dating in many ways. By combining effective hypnotherapy and NLP (Neuro Linguistic Programming) skills, we are getting amazing results!

Many of my clients, who hadn't been on the dating scene for a while and were a bit "rusty" after being in a long relationship or marriage, wanted some tools to utilize in their daily life.

Some men needed assistance in upgrading their image, while others wanted a female opinion on making their home or apartment appropriate for romance and love. I took men shopping to create a winning image and then worked on the inside — helping them to upgrade their belief systems to match the new exterior image they were creating. This gave them a winning combination of power and confidence both inside and out! Even married men will benefit despite the fact that this book was geared for single men. Perhaps by treating your relationship like you did when you were dating you can revive your marriage and your soul!

This book contains all the basic details women wish men would learn and apply to their lives. *Love Mechanics* is not just about relationships with women, it's also about building a relationship with yourself. You'll be preparing yourself first and developing a closer relationship with women in the process. **You'll become the man every woman wants!**

Love Mechanics is the first in a series that will walk you through the simple steps to prepare for love in a language you can relate to.

You will begin with the internal diagnosis of your phases in life, the vibrations you send out, and how to get control of your life by being in tune with your goals. You will then be guided through the internal and external checklists that make it simple to understand the actions to take to prepare for a relationship. This complete tune-up can save you years of research on topics you may have wanted to explore but didn't have the time to. I have done it all for you! You will learn to observe, to listen and to recognize energy — from yourself and others — to see if you are a match.

Then by adding some powerful techniques used in NLP, you will learn the science and the art of how we use our mind to communicate with ourselves and others. You will learn simple ways to use your brain deliberately and shift beliefs you have about yourself that affect your life and experiences. By learning to build rapport, becoming aware of the primary communication styles of others and how our words affect them, you will have the nuts and bolts to build a connection to yourself and take responsibility for your life. In doing so, you will tune into why you're connecting — or not connecting — to the people in your life. Especially women!

Certainly, with the Internet connecting people worldwide, there are many opportunities to express our desires on a screen, but what I hear from singles out there is that it's another picture when they meet in person. People are different face-to-face. The "energy" isn't the same as online. It still remains that people have to meet in person after the connection is established and discuss their desires and goals and hope to make a connection. A first impression is a lasting one and can be a deal breaker for both sexes.

You'll discover the best places to meet available women, learn the clear signals to know if you have a green or red light. You'll be a man with a winning plan!

Let's begin your tune-up now! Be open and honest with yourself to obtain maximum results. From my heart and soul to yours…go for it and you <u>will</u> create success with women, with your life…and have a lot of fun in the meantime! Are you ready?

PART ONE
THE INTERNAL TUNE-UP

VEHICLE IDENTIFICATION

"The unexamined life is not worth living."

-Plato

WHAT CONDITION ARE YOU IN?

Let's get started. In Chapter 1, we will assess your current condition as a single man. You are the vehicle that we will be tuning up, and it begins by examining the current phase of your life and the dating situations you may be experiencing now. We will uncover the phase or phases you are presently going through, acknowledging that you're the one behind the wheel, then you will decide whether you will stay put or move on.

We all go through many different phases in single life. You need to be *honest* with yourself now about what phase you are in, so you can move ahead, achieve your goals and deepen the connection to your own life and soul. Your current phase determines the necessary actions and the appropriate tuning to get you back on the road.

You must be clear and honest with yourself and others when you are out connecting, or you might be led on or confused. At least if you know what the *truth* is and tell the *truth*, all parties can make a choice to get involved or not.

Just like choosing a vehicle, you look at where you are at in your life and what your needs are, then you can check out all your options. The same goes for relationships. I'm surprised that so many people who attend my classes are numb to this. When asked, *"When it comes to your love life, what are you looking for right now?"*, their answers are all over the road. *"Love? Maybe. I'm not sure. A friend? A companion? I just want casual sex. Just to get out again seems like a hassle! Takes too much time right now, but I would like to date occasionally. Marriage — not for me right now, I'm building my company!"*

Many people aren't clear on their goals in relationships, so they keep attracting situations that cause unnecessary stress in their life, or they have no action at all and they wonder why. When you send out mixed signals, you get mixed results!

STOP NOW! Ask yourself if you even know your place in the game. Most of us go through phases where we are open, loving and creative. Then some single men get so negative, shutdown and shell-shocked that no one could penetrate them with love if they tried. Sometimes you are ready to dive into the depths of passion and love from your core. At other times you are focused, growing and exploring your life alone. Ask yourself; *"Where am I as a single man? Am I just out looking for casual sex? Do I want to lease or buy long-term? Do I know enough about what I want in a relationship?"* So many single men are frustrated because they don't know why they are creating havoc in their single existence. They are so desperately seeking love, picking the wrong partners or avoiding pain with drinking, smoking, sex, drugs, pornography...wondering why their love life isn't working or why they are all alone.

By becoming more conscious of your current status, you can design and plan the steps you are willing to take to move forward. There will be many insights along the way to uplift and shift your pattern in relationships. You're in the driver's seat from now on.

WHAT PHASE ARE YOU IN?

Each phase is broken down so that you can do an honest evaluation of your current situation as a single man. You will also become aware of the phases that women you date go through. This is where many men get off track because they may be in a phase that isn't congruent with the person (or people) they are dating and pretend that they can handle the situation. Frankly, it's just as important to know their phases as it is your own.

When there is honesty and clarity right from the start it will keep the record straight, so we can all steer clear of unnecessary pain and create what we deeply desire. Some of the important values in creating a strong foundation for relationships are honesty and integrity. Many of us aren't even honest with ourselves, let alone with the people we date. Read on, and then utilize this information to get clear signals to see if you really have a **Green** light to go forward ◀️🎱▶️. Sometimes we don't read the signs properly, and we should be **Yielding** ▽ or coming to a complete **Stop** 🛑. Let's explore the phases and take note of the reminder signs along the way.

SHOCK ABSORPTION ▽

Are you in shock after a long-term relationship — or marriage — and suddenly single again? New to the game? All shook up about being out there on your own? Suddenly you're in the situation where your mate moved away or transferred, or abruptly left the relationship, or maybe you broke it off realizing you weren't a good match for a long-term relationship?

This is surely a time of healing and growth, and depending on the type of separation, there is a necessary adjustment period to be fully ready to move on to another relationship. Getting adjusted to living alone or not having that other person around takes time to absorb the shock.

This phase can be very painful and feels like a divorce — whether it was or not. Even if you weren't married, the bonding was there, and the disappointment can rake at your heart. At other times, you feel relieved and excited about your new status and welcome the freedom to explore new relationships.

From a woman's standpoint, meeting you right now can be difficult, because even if you broke it off, you still have to go through a separation period from the other person's energy, from the old life-style and from habits you shared. Consider taking a time-out to recover, instead of jumping back on the freeway and trying to find someone right away. Many men who are "suddenly single" go on a quest for knowledge to learn from their relationship so as not to repeat the past. I assist many singles in this phase and suggest that you get support to grow into your new life style slowly with kindness and openness.

Depending on how you look at it, this can either be a time of difficulty and challeng or of great excitement. If you don't heal the past before starting to date again, you could become embittered and give up or repeat unhealthy patterns. **STAY OPEN.** This book offers you healing tools and will help you discover many ways to recharge yourself. Hang in there! Being suddenly single is usually a blessing in disguise.

Take a deep breath and relax.

LOW PRESSURE

In the low-pressure phase, you are either uninterested in a long-term relationship or don't have the desire to be with one woman at this time. Perhaps you are new to dating or just beginning to adjust to your new single status. Maybe you have done some healing, and you desire to just hang out and be friends with new people. You're checking out your options. You enjoy dating various women, and you may or may not be sexually intimate with different women. Whatever your state of mind, you don't want any pressure and truthfully you still want to explore your options.

If you are having casual sex and know for sure your partner wants more, you must be clear in your communication. If this is you, *be honest* with the women you are dating. You can save your partners a lot of heartache, and you will also not have the guilt many men carry around knowing that they won't go for the "long haul" with this woman. If you know a woman wants more, and she wants to jump in too fast, slow down and proceed with open communication, build the foundation first and tell her the truth to avoid pain later. Women tell me that the evasiveness is what drives them crazy. We want honesty so we know our options. Don't play with other people's hearts and souls!

Some men will know they are leading a woman on and, because they don't want to lose out on the sex, they may pretend the relationship is happening. This situation happens often, and many women feel betrayed. Be fair - don't lie just to have sex. A very attractive man I met was dating a single mother with a three year-old child and knew he never intended to marry her, and yet he kept the relationship going because he didn't feel like "hurting" her and he didn't want to give up the sex. Believe me, telling a woman in the early phases is better than dragging her into a supposed "relationship" and having her feel hurt later on. What a selfish man to keep his options open and yet make her believe she is "the one."

Some women only want casual sex themselves, and if both parties are clear and honest, you'd be surprised at how many women are open to this phase. Discuss it...don't assume you know the real deal unless you have asked! Men can get hurt too!

Also, I strongly suggest taking it easy if you're dating a woman who tells you that this is the phase she is experiencing and you want more. Believe her! Go slow and take caution. *Pay attention* to the signs along the way, especially if you are in a different phase and looking for more than a casual date or sex. Listen to the verbal messages and use your intuition. Men often get bonded by sex, and many of my clients experience women who just want to play. They fell in love with a woman who told them the truth up front but they didn't listen. Open up your ears guys! In these wild times, honesty is the best policy.

PASSENGERS STILL IN YOUR VEHICLE

You appear to be single but you still have a lover in your heart that you haven't quite let go of. You may have broken off a relationship and are "just friends" with your ex or you may still be having sex with her for fear of being alone. You may consider yourself to be back in the market, but you'll never be fully present for anyone else with your old lover's energy hanging around. It's like having a pile of garbage in your car — no one else can take a ride until it is cleaned out. You truly have a person remaining in your vehicle – in your heart that is. The space isn't free. You haven't let go.

Having someone in the wings can block you from new love, and dating you can be frustrating for those who desire deeper intimacy. Be honest with others you're dating about this other woman and your situation in order to grant them their fair options. Don't be selfish! There is nothing worse than dating someone who pretends they are over someone. At first they want to just play around, then when sex and intimate situations come up, their heartache will surface. If you're dating someone like this, you may not even be aware of the lack of presence until you have dated for some time. You'll sense that they have energy somewhere else, and you're not sure why. I've had clients whose dates were still living with "old partners." Of course, my clients were constantly feeling confused because they were not a priority. If you sense that something is amiss, look for signs of someone else in her life, such as moodiness, inconsistent behavior, secret phone calls and broken plans. Use your intuition on this one and ask for clarity.

One client had always had a man named Mark in her life that she felt very strongly about. She never got to explore the relationship due to distance and timing in their lives. Each time a new man came into her life, she would only be halfway in the relationship because Mark remained in her heart and thoughts. Mark would call often to keep the flame alive, but they weren't in a real relationship. When she came to me for coaching, she became aware that by having the incomplete communication with Mark she would never move forward with any other man. She was living in the fantasy of "someday." Instead of dragging her new "friend" into a relationship that was unfulfilling, she needed to detach from Mark first or explore this fantasy relationship once and for all. By leaving it open and unclear, her heart was torn between two lovers! She needed to rid herself of the energy of Mark in her heart. Once she did clear out this old relationship, she was free to truly love her new man. He came to me also and said the whole time they were together he felt that this other man's presence was ruining the intimacy with her. He supported her in the process to clean up her life by giving her the time and space to let go of Mark, and now they are together, committed and sharing a deeper connection than ever.

Do you have a passenger still remaining in your vehicle?

COMPLETE ENGINE BREAKDOWN

If you are in the Complete Engine Breakdown phase, you have had a bad breakup. You are a single soul who is depressed, irate, or shut down. Possibly, you experience all of these symptoms from time to time. You no longer believe in love, perhaps you even hate women. You are completely in a rut.

You are constantly focused on hurts from the past. You say things like *"Why bother? Dating is a pain in the neck. I'm never going to love again. I'm fed up with women."* Some men (and women) in this phase try to fill that void with work, partying, sex, drugs, gambling, food or drinking, while others go into long states of depression and grief.

Whatever your activities, you aren't willing to take responsibility for being on the merry-go-round of negative consciousness — round and round you go with your anger, your actions, your words, and your core beliefs. Being around you is challenging, especially if others are in a happy state. It irritates you.

If you are in this phase, your energy can easily drive others away. Keep reading and learn how to change that energy and create a fulfilling single life.

TIMING ADJUSTMENTS ▽

You're a newly divorced father or a single parent. You may be feeling sad and vulnerable, perplexed that the breakup happened. Conversely, you may be relieved of the burden of "the ex" and enthralled to be moving on! A friend of mine said it was like his parole was over and he was free. Don't be fooled, healing is happening whether you want to admit it or not. Having children involved adds to the adjustment time, the energy drain, and the stress.

Being a single parent is a lot of work. Moreover, it takes patience and communication to work out the custody details and schedules for the care of the children. Their emotions — and lifestyles — are impacted, so it is very important to put the children's interests first no matter what you're dealing with in the process.

Men show up in my classes newly separated from a longtime partner, shell-shocked and, in my opinion, not in a great place to create a safe foundation with a new partner. To my surprise, other men in their situation are very sensitive and in search of a support system for their new situation. I tell them to reach out for support and begin building a new network if they don't have friends for support!

Any way you slice it, this phase isn't easy. You're in a phase that can take some time to repair, and your situation is unique to you and your particular set of circumstances. You have to separate your things, move and regroup. Money issues and custody challenges take a lot of energy and adjustment time for everyone. You may be experiencing some pain, sorrow, and disappointment. This book will be a guide for you to mend your heart and tune-up before you get back out on the road.

On the other side of the coin, meeting a freshly divorced woman is okay, but move slowly. Otherwise you may end up being the healing angel who is left in the parking lot alone after the woman gets back into balance.

SECURING YOUR VEHICLE

You're in the foundation phase, focused on building your career, setting goals for your future, and achieving them step by step. You're very committed to security and may not have time to nurture a full-time relationship. You're securing your vehicle: laying the cornerstones for your life and creating your empire.

People do desire to have a partner and to build a future together in this phase. If you do meet someone who wants a relationship, it is imperative to be honest, to let her know if you're too busy with your career. She may be in a similar situation, or she can provide you with the support you need during this important phase in your life. Learn your unique communication style and hers to maintain good communication, otherwise you're liable to cause a lot of distress. Planning and communication are essential.

HIGH PERFORMANCE

You're an on-the-go businessman working round the clock. You have a strong commitment to your work and your personal goals — you have a lot to watch over. You're already successful and have to maintain it.

If this describes you, you may find it challenging to get out to date or to meet new people, because your energy is focused on work, work, work. Because of the high performance and steady maintenance it takes to stay on top, women in your life must be patient. Dating you can be very frustrating, because you're driven by money, power, competition and success. Usually, when powerful, highly intelligent men like this desire to relax and play, they want an understanding, undemanding partner who appreciates all the hard work they've done and are doing now!

The problem arises when your goal-focused life-style clashes with the needs and desires of the woman in your life. You must help her see that it is not personal. The fact is, you are on a quest. She may be part of your support team and your inspiration, or she may be on her own path to success. This High Performance syndrome goes both ways. The times have changed, and women work just as long and hard as men these days. Balancing work, home, kids and a man can be stressful.

Many High Performance people marry, sharing their lives and growing together, and as long as there is clear understanding, good ongoing communication and lots of appreciation — it can work!

However, when men are too focused on work, and the women in their lives feel under-appreciated and under-nurtured, the romance can definitely fade. Hundreds of women surveyed mentioned that their husbands/boyfriends work too much and that they miss the romance and quality time. They are happy for the success of their men, but what is it all for? To live at the office? To never have time to enjoy the money? This is a serious challenge for many successful couples in our society today.

Is this you? If so, wake up! There will always be an *"important meeting,"* the next *"really big deal,"* and, of course, the promises to take a few days off *"soon."*

Are you:

- *Constantly busy?*
- *Working on days off?*
- *Eating on the run?*
- *Always rushing?*
- *Thinking about work on vacation (which you sometimes cut short)?*
- *Hearing a lot of complaints (about you) from those closest in your life?*
- *Having little or no intimacy?*

Some single men get caught up in work so they don't have to deal with loneliness or the time it takes to create relationships. Perhaps they don't see intimacy, developing or maintaining a relationship as a priority. Sometimes years will pass. Their lives become all about work. I meet many men in my seminars whose wives or lovers left them for this reason. The men still wonder why. Their typical comment is: *"I made tons of money she had it all— what else does she want?"* or *"Love is too much work. I have enough on my plate right now." HELLO!!!*

If you don't want to end up rich and alone, consider creating a shift in your life. Unless, of course, that is what you choose for yourself. Only you know what is in your heart. Ask yourself:

- *Am I using my accomplishments to get noticed?*
- *Am I trying to prove something to someone?*
- *What motivates me to work so much?*
- *Am I working to numb my emotions or to cover insecurity or pain?*
- *Did I dig myself into a situation I can't dig myself out of? Is there a solution in sight?*
- *Is the work giving me the satisfaction I deserve?*
- *Am I happy and balanced in other areas of my life — romance, friendships, family time?*
- *Do I want a relationship now and am I willing to attend to my partner's needs?*
- *Am I afraid of intimacy? Have I ever been intimate?*
- *Am I willing to slow down a bit NOW to achieve more balance in my current situation?*
- *What steps can I take to move forward to create a social life?*

We live in a fast-paced world, but we must maintain a balance to have some sanity in our lives. If you're a High Performance type, you must create space and time to have love and intimacy or in the end, your accomplishments will mean nothing to you.

BURNING RUBBER

In my interviews with numerous students, I've been told that the challenges of school and work don't allow for much socializing. Students feel that they are constantly on the run — burning rubber from their jobs to school to the study hall! If you're a student, I'm sure you know what I'm talking about. In this day and age, thousands of us are back in school to get an advanced degree while still working. It can be hard to connect with your classmates, but it is important to take a few hours a week to meet new people.

If you're dating a student, you won't be the priority for a while, but it's not impossible to create time for social interaction — and hopefully some love and intimacy. If both parties understand the process, go forward and co-create a winning relationship.

Some students have great social skills, while the left-brainers who have studied for years need to get back into balance after school has ended. The divorce rate of doctors, surgeons, engineers, and lawyers is quite high. This is largely due to the high stress and long hours of required study, which all but eliminates socializing time and developing people skills during those grueling hours at medical, law or business school. Many highly educated professionals attend my seminars to brush up on people skills never taught in universities.

Keep reading, you're in the right place.

These days, many people are waiting longer to get married, developing their careers before jumping into the long-term commitment phase of life. These tools will be a strong foundation for you to create heathier relationships in all areas of your life.

ROAD MAP

You're new to the area and don't know your way around. Where are the great hangouts, the hot groups, the exciting events? At first, you may only know co-workers or fellow students and you're anxious to find your niche here in your new home. Of course, it can be exciting to explore, but it takes time, especially in big cities.

Depending on your reasons for moving and the current status of your heart, you could be having the adventure of a lifetime. If you're still healing from a relationship or are separated from your current lover, we will tune you up! In the following chapters, I'll suggest ways to plug into your new area that will help you create new directions in your life. No worries!

HIGH-SPEED CHASER ▽

You're sleek and on the run. You jump from one new deal to another — always ready to try out the slicker model. The thrill of the ride excites you. You don't want attachment. You don't want commitment. If you do make commitments for a long-term relationship, you don't keep them. You lease yourself out and go for a quick trade-in when the ride gets uncomfortable.

You're like a knight in shining armor riding from castle to castle. You don't give details, just vague and charming stories. You desire different partners for hot sex and love to show off your latest conquest to your friends. You never know where you will end up or with whom. You don't keep promises and rarely make them.

If you do have friends, they're just like you. From the outside, your life appears glamorous. You're always on the scene, always looking good. Of course, this phase can be very exciting, yet may be damaging other people along the way.

You're having a ball, but your playing can hurt the people you date if you're not honest about what is real for you.

Some "bad boys" will admit to being in this phase. Deep inside they have huge egos and need to be validated constantly. Women in this phase need the same kind of approval, so they tend to find High-Speed Chasers to temporarily fill the void.

A High-Speed Chaser can't live without the thrill, the attention and the false confidence that one partner after another gives him. Usually singles in the early years of dating are in this phase, but some people never grow out of it, especially in cities where there are lots of beautiful people (i.e., Los Angeles, New York, Dallas, Atlanta). If you are a high-speed chaser, let women know it up front and be honest so you don't wound innocent women with your deception. These "white" lies can cause women to distrust men that want the "real deal" in the future.

Your influence and power with women can cause lifelong pain and heart damage that takes years to undo. Go easy on the younger, more vulnerable women, because you could be the man that creates the first love experience for her young impressionable soul. Your power and looks are gifts to be used with honor, respect and dignity.

Many of these types of men I have interviewed on my TV shows admit that deep inside they felt guilty when they knew the women were falling in love with them and that they had no intention of following up or being committed to them. They pursued those women for the thrill factor using what they knew she wanted to "hear" to get her in bed. Then off to the next thrill leaving her damaged in the meantime and never looking back. I'm here to tell you your actions do have an impact on women. Have a positive influence on women's lives by using your gifts with honor. Tell the truth and save yourself the guilt and save the women heartbreak.

There are many women these days that are out looking for the same thrill. If you're dating a woman in this phase, have fun — that's about all you'll have. It's a fast and furious short-lived ride. Be aware of your heart if you want more!

If you're after deeper intimacy, don't go there — it's a waste of time!

COMFORTABLE RIDE

You've finally let go of your last relationship and you're enjoying a comfortable ride. You are a happy, free agent and can do whatever you want, whenever you want with no residual pain from the past. Most singles come to this place when the healing process is finished. In the Comfortable Ride phase, you've shifted gears to a new level about what you deserve, you're out again and feeling good. It's a great place to be.

You know when you go out with a woman that she isn't IT! You're dating new people, but you're not looking for a long-term ride at this time.

The Comfortable Ride phase holds an important key to creating your future. When old, past patterns resurface, now you know how to process through them. So have fun, drop unrealistic expectations, and explore new friends. Stay focused, keep working on yourself during this time and you will consistently create new opportunities and connections with interesting prospects.

When you're in the Comfortable Ride phase, you are living in the now and your heart is open. Feel the freedom of your spirit and explore with joy!

UNDER-THE-HOOD ▼

This is a phase of exploration into your soul. It comes when you realize you haven't reached your goals in love and in life.

Perhaps you're in a relationship that isn't consistent with who you are now – you have grown, you're yearning to connect with the deeper parts of yourself. You can't pretend not to hear the truth any longer. Your inner voice is speaking, and you know it's time to take a look under the hood, to see your underlying challenges, and willingly undergo a tune-up.

In the Under-the-Hood phase, you connect with a more profound inner life, and you may want to share these new explorations with your friends and/or your current partner. Perhaps you can save your relationship if you were to go deeper?

You may want to consult with a therapist and check out what is the basis for your concerns. Many men have a conflict here: they think it's feminine to go deep into themselves, and yet they yearn to experience more intimacy. Be open! Ask for assistance!

RIDING SOLO ▼

You've been single for so long that you wonder if you are able to fit someone into your life. You're in a groove, you have a free life-style, and you can come and go as you please. You have a distant dream of meeting someone who could merge with your life, but your vision isn't clear yet as to how that could happen. You're afraid that you will have to compromise your current *modus operandi.*

You enjoy riding solo. It will take the real deal to break you out of your routine. Your standards may be set so high that you make it impossible for anyone to fit in. If you want to be with a woman, you will have to break some habits and alter comfortable routines — and this seems all-but-impossible right now. You see what it takes to develop and maintain a soul-mate relationship and you wonder, *Can I ever have a relationship and be happy?*

The only way to know is to explore relationships with an open mind. Potential partners may say you are selfish and think only of yourself. Is it true? Do you make partners jump through hoops to override the barriers to your heart? Are you commitment-phobic? If so, this can lead those who are involved with you into the Out-of-Gas phase.

OUT-OF-GAS

You have dated casually but have never gone deep into a relationship, so you're just giving up on the whole idea for yourself. Perhaps you have never had a real "relationship" or you keep attracting commitment-phobic or unavailable people. Because of past rejections or lack of connection, you may feel unworthy to have love. Maybe you feel you don't deserve it. You never quite believed in love, and you've lived out your beliefs in most of your dating scenarios. More than likely, you didn't have any role models to guide you. You feel shutdown and alienated. At least on the surface, you've accepted your fate: you were *born* alone, and you'll *stay* alone.

Nevertheless, the desire for deep connection is buried inside your heart and soul. You just don't know how to find it.

If this is you, cheer up! There are many ways to get out of this dark phase and create a new attitude about life. This is a new territory for you. No worries! Keep reading.

TIMING IS OFF

If you are in this phase, the timing just does not flow. For reasons of location, educational obligations, work, previous commitments, etc., the people involved are out of sync. It can be painful if the person is right but the timing is off, but you can't force anything. Perhaps in the future it could work, but don't live your life waiting for someone else to come through for you. If it is meant to happen, it will.

Until then, live life to the fullest! Move on and don't take it personally.

NO HEAT COMBUSTION

In this phase you may be dating someone who is attractive, wonderful, caring and the perfect type to connect with, but there is no chemistry. Either one or the other person just doesn't feel the magic or the heat you'd like to experience long- term, yet there is a connection. You may have been attempting dating for awhile to see if it could "heat" up and it never progresses. You may have gotten involved romantically too soon (under the influence of alcohol or drugs) and now you wish you could back out. This phase is uncomfortable for all parties concerned and honest communication is a must! Sometimes these people can become friends if the parties involved handle this phase with care and loving honest communication. Some space and time may be needed when separating to accept the phase for what it is. I always say…*"If it ain't flowing, it ain't going."* Move on!

CONSTANT REPAIR

In the Constant Repair phase, you are continually searching for answers from outside yourself. Not that the search isn't great — you're reading this, aren't you? At some point you must _STOP_ looking and actually apply the information that you discovered. Do the work on yourself before trying out the newest seminar or quick fix. I watch too many people attend my seminars, eager and enthusiastic, then lose momentum by not using the tune-up tools. You must make a road map first to find which direction you want to travel in and then take steps in that direction. There are no quick fixes or temporary repairs. Take the necessary time to do the self-repair. Do the work daily and be consistent, and you will get powerful results.

Follow-up on your new adventure, and both your trip and your arrival at your chosen destination will be well worth it!

FUEL DRAINER

If you're in the Fuel Drainer Phase, you feel so desperate to find someone that you will do *anything* for love. You will cling and hang onto the slightest glimmer of hopeful connection. You will have chronic health problems, eating disorders, or serious money challenges. You will have addictions to alcohol, drugs and cigarettes. You will be constantly asking for help. In bold print, your calling card will say, **"co-dependent."**

If you are in this phase, you may want to get more help, and some of the guidelines in this book will assist you in finding the right healing modality for you. Then you can develop a healthy foundation from which to work.

DEAD END STREET

You've been dating someone for a long time (2 years or more) and know for sure that you won't marry this person. You want to break up, but you don't want to deal with the loneliness or with the singles scene. You are not telling the truth about what is happening in your relationship for fear of hurting her. Believe me, she will be more hurt if you allow it to go on for too much longer! Tell the truth and let go! Don't turn your life or hers down a dead end street.

TOP RUNNING CONDITION

Top Running Condition is the place to be! You're finally in a zone where you accept yourself. You've defined your personal and relationship values and you appreciate yourself for the gift you are. You are fulfilled being single and open to meeting others who are in similar states.

To be in Top Running Condition does not mean you want to stay single, only that you have created yourself to be *what you are asking for*. You are *"THE ONE."* You are committed to your life purpose and to living in the moment, seeing both yourself and others with a deeper vision. You are now demonstrating an inner trust in your own soul for guiding you to the perfect friendships, relationships, and love in all areas of your life. Your energy emanates confidence, self-esteem, and wisdom.

You move about your life in "Top Running Condition" until you magnetize your match or are fulfilled being alone.

LONG-TERM CONNECTION

If you're in this phase, you've been on the solo-journey long enough. You're ready to commit to a relationship and you're looking for a quality long-term connection. You've explored your options and are prepared to take off on a new trail with a mate. You want to create a bonding with that special someone and travel down the path of love.

You're ready for the long haul. You understand women. You know what they bring to enhance and enliven your life and what gifts you have to share in a partnership. You're ready to explore the world with an evolved partner, knowing there will be ups and downs, and to co-create a life that is unique to your common vision.

Now that we have checked out our current single status, it's time to see what energy we emit to others, which leads us to....

VEHICLE VIBRATION 2

"What a man thinketh, so shall he become!"

--James Allen

WHAT MESSAGE ARE YOU SENDING TO OTHERS?

Now that we've explored the phase you're moving through as a single man, we need to check the energy you're sending out. This is the next key for becoming consciously responsible for how we are showing up in the world. The energy that some people walk around with is horrifying and downright cold. It's as if a cloud of depression and indifference keeps people from connecting.

We live in a fast-paced, modern world and we want things done quickly. We make instant connections with people by e-mail, fax and cell phone. The answering machine has dehumanized the telephone — which had already dehumanized personal connection. (A recent survey revealed that most of us just hate it when people actually answer the phone; all we want to do is leave the message on the machine!) What's missing in all of this is the kind of *ENERGY* that can be transmitted person to person. We're all communicating faster, easier, and more effectively, but guess what? The absence of personal connection is leaving millions of us home alone playing with our mouses instead of our spouses.

Let's face it – single life is all over the map. At times, being single is as lonely as it gets, and sometimes it's the wildest of adventures, but at all times it provides the opportunity to see what we really desire and to make smart choices for ourselves. These choices begin with our energy state. This new electronic age has incredible benefits to society, but it brings with it a disastrous side effect. Our one-on-one communication is getting shut down. There is already much scientific research on all of this "energy" information and more surfaces weekly. You'll be able to read more in my upcoming book series.

Regardless of your circumstances, your energy vibe will absolutely influence your outcomes. You are exquisitely unique and wonderfully complex, and as you become laser honest with yourself and with others, you can take charge of your life and make healthier choices. You can create what you really want. This is the second step in your tuning: to become more aware of the energy and messages you're putting out in the world. Only you know what vibe you're in. Be brutally honest with yourself, and remember, this book isn't here to judge you, just to give you a wake-up call.

How many times have you entered an event or party and immediately scanned the room to see if anyone there was your "type"? If your "scanner" picks up a receptive energy, like a magnet you're drawn in, because you can sense an emanating energy that you want around you. Usually it is a physical "type" we look for, and most of the time we don't connect because our personal frequencies aren't in sync. If your energies are on different frequencies, and you do connect, it won't be for long.

You might get a chance to meet, but you won't be welcomed into her "space," because one of the two of you will move on. That's how it is with energy. Even when you're in control of it and you send out great vibes, you have experiences that don't jive. You can't take it personally. They aren't on the same frequency, so why waste your time with them? The automatic judgments and egos of some people are impossible to penetrate. They may look like your type and yet the frequency is way off, so move on. Who wants to be with a cold, negative-energy person in the first place?

Like everyone else, you have times in your life when you're inspired; you're having a great day; you're on top of the world. Everything is going right, you're feeling good inside, and you're in the flow! People notice you. Maybe even a woman you think is "hot" talks or connects with you. Suddenly, doubt creeps in and you wonder, *"What's up, why would she look at me?"* Something inside gets triggered. You go back into a funk, and that magic "feeling" disappears. The questions begin: *"How did I get that inspiration? How can I get it again? Come back to me!!!"* Finally, you say to yourself, *"Oh well, back to normal."*

Now, being depressed and staying in that funk is not normal, but it feels natural to many of us, right? Many singles are so used to feeling miserable, they think that's how it's supposed to be. Who told you that lie? Life is what you make it to be, and you are in charge!

You can shift out of that mindset when you figure out the energy you're sending out. You're in the driver's seat. You're in control. I promise you that the work you do on this will change your life dramatically — in all areas. Many of my students report instant success with others by facing themselves and shifting their energy vibe.

Energy is all around us. If you tune in a little, you can sense energy-draining and energy-producing vibrations from every aspect of your environment, be it nature, music, media, the people you surround yourself with and your home environment.

In the rest of this chapter, you will become aware of what vibrations you send out. This awareness will take honesty and will shift your relationships with lovers, friends, family, business associates — and especially, with yourself.

THE VIBRATION OF YOUR VEHICLE

Although you have a unique vibration, you can fluctuate between these vibrations at different times in your life. As you become aware of which vibration you send out, you can shift gears to a higher frequency, thus creating a new life. This process takes time and awareness.

Awareness of the energies you put out is the second step to shifting yourself and magnetizing or reigniting more love into your life. Once you see what vibes you send out, you can catch yourself and shift gears! Let's check into your Energy Vibes and see in which state you are living!

ENERGY VIBES

THE ANGRY VIBER: A scowling face is the calling card of the Angry Viber. An Angry Viber is filled with wrath, explosive energy and impatience. You can feel his rage and annoyance from across the room. His movements are sharp: Whap!, he will snap if the wrong thing is said.

THE BALANCED VIBER: The Balanced Viber has the ultimate balance of inner peace and harmony. His life reflects stability, poise, and balance in all areas. He radiates a sense of inner tranquility that we all strive for.

THE CODEPENDENT VIBER: This caregiver thinks of others first but can be very needy. Codependent Vibers give, give and give to feel loved — then feel taken for granted. His giving is a trade-off for approval and validation. He has a tendency to rehash his problems on the phone, overanalyzing every word to figure out what he did wrong. He can be whiny and have mood swings.

THE CONFIDENT LEADER VIBER: This person radiates confidence and power, a presence that others are drawn to magically. A self-assured, vibrant and positive vibe is one we all strive for.

A man with this courageous leadership vibration is a good role model.

THE CONTROL-FREAK VIBER: Control is the name of his game. Bossy and demanding, he tries to command people's time, energy, and sometimes other's beliefs. In his presence, people feel manipulated. He desires to take the lead and govern activities, and he definitely gets upset when things don't go his way.

THE DAMAGED VIBER: This sensitive person is like a bird with a broken wing, in the process of healing, searching to learn from his lessons in order to fly again. To the outside world, the Damaged Viber comes across like damaged goods.

THE DEAD-ENGINE VIBER: A Dead Engine sends out no energy, is slow moving, has slumped shoulders, a monotone voice, sad eyes, is in a depressed state most of the time, and looks like the walking dead. If this is you, check your pulse.

THE DECEPTIVE VIBER: This type doesn't tell the truth and most often he doesn't keep commitments. Misleading and cunning, he doesn't look people straight in the eye during important or stressful conversations. He has a shifty, insincere way about him and can deceive others with stories.

THE HIGH VIBER: This person is usually extroverted, stands tall with his shoulders back, walks on air, smiles a lot and connects well with others. A High Viber is most often a leader and/or an entrepreneurial type. He is strong, energetic and lighthearted, and can be impatient and pushy at times. He can come across phony to those with low energy and at the same time he can be the life of the party that everyone notices.

THE HIGH-STRUNG VIBER: A High-Strung Viber is a frenetic, nervous person who rarely calms down. Being around him makes others want to jump out of their skin. He has sharp, quick movements — like a free-flying electrical wire — that can burn out energy.

THE HORN-DOG VIBER: This person seems slimy and sends out a perverted, twisted vibe that is scary to women. He may stalk women, stare at body parts and he has no respect for personal space. Like the Sexual Viber, he sends out signals of desperation. It is a turnoff!

THE IMPATIENT VIBER: This person can't sit still. He is tense, restless, and he want things now! He is impulsive, a harried decision-maker and can be challenging to be in a relationship with for those who have calming energy.

THE JEALOUS VIBER: The Jealous Viber is so possessive and domineering that you feel restricted from looking at another human when you are in his presence. He controls people with his energy which is rooted in deep insecurity and fear.

THE JOKER VIBER: The Joker Viber uses his humor to connect and is constantly telling stories and making zany wisecracks to get attention and to meet people. He is loud, sometimes obnoxious and attracts a lot of attention. He is fun to be around, and women who love to laugh will be attracted and entertained by him. Many of these jesters wear their humor like a mask to keep from taking anything seriously. If this describes you, I want you to realize that the jokes you tell reflect your self-image and reveal your focus in life — especially when first connecting with people.

THE KIND VIBER: Warm, sparkling eyes and a graceful stance and walk are sure signs of the Kind Viber. He will have open energy, is captivating, considerate, and a pleasure to be around. He emanates love and glows when he enters a room.

THE LITTLE-BOY VIBER: The playful, fun energy of the Little-Boy Viber is compelling at first, but ultimately the Little Boy turns out to be undependable, irresponsible and reckless. He wants to act like a child who doesn't know better, but he's actually looking for someone to take care of him. Some men never grow up, and dating a Little Boy can be draining. It is great to get in touch with your "inner child" and be playful, as long as you are responsible in the other areas of your life.

THE MAMA'S BOY-VIBER: Overpowering, controlling mothers have brought up some men who can't release the hold these women have over their lives. He checks in with Mom or women friends for every decision and carries around guilt or shame when it comes to certain situations with women. The Mama's Boy has not let go of the attachment to his mother and may have an unhealthy relationship with women because of the deep desire to recreate his mother in the women he chooses. Some of these men look to be with "control freak" women and marry someone just like Mom.

This issue has become prevalent in our current times due to the increased divorce rate. Because of this and other related reasons, there are many books written on this subject.

THE MONEY-HUNGRY VIBER: The Money-Hungry Viber is focused on having a ton of money and high status. He cares about materialistic things and how much they cost. His worth may be measured by how much he spent on something. He asks many questions to find out the financial status of friends and potential partners and can pry into others lives in a very subtle way. Usually, he is very good at deceiving people and will offer to assist people in business and with their personal issues so he can get a foothold in their affairs. Watch out, this person can be very shifty.

THE NARCISSISTIC VIBER: This dynamic person is on a power trip. He's puffed up, cocky and always boasting: "And I did this, then I did that, then I did this again…" Narcissistic Vibers need a lot of attention and are willing to be louder than the crowd to get it. He wants his ego stroked a lot. A Narcissistic Viber's only focus is me, me, me. He is egocentric, vain, intense and full of himself. He will only do things that benefit him! His energy emanates selfishness and smugness.

THE NEEDY VIBER: This person comes across as extremely needy and may be pushy because he is so desperate for love. The needy person himself doesn't have a life of his own and tends to attach to people who have their lives together. He will offer help and assistance and drain people's energy when he dumps his problems with a full dose of whining. This vibe can be felt in the tone of his voice or in conversations when he talks about old relationships or lack thereof.

THE NERDY VIBER: The Nerdy energy comes across as uncomfortable, bashful, and socially challenged. His look is not together and he seems to be the poster boy for rejection. Nerdy Vibers are shy, lack confidence and can be introverted.

THE OPEN-HEART VIBER: Open-Heart Viber loves life and people. You can feel tenderness from him when he interacts with you. He is warm and caring, and he will maintain good eye contact.

THE PEACEFUL VIBER: A mellow, reflective, intuitive, soft-spoken person who has a tranquil and healing effect. Women will feel serene in his presence. They move with a stride of inner strength and confidence.

THE PROTECTIVE VIBER: This defensive person has a wall of protection so thick that if a person gets too close he might lash out at them. Or he is completely closed off for fear of being hurt. He tends to get very snappy, and has a tone of defensiveness in his voice. The Protective Viber is safeguarding and shielding his heart.

THE RECEPTIVE VIBER: This is an interested man sending clear signals that he has open, approachable energy. From the warm look in his eyes and his body language, a woman knows immediately that he is hospitable and responsive. He smiles a lot and makes great eye contact. He acknowledges her comments and laughs easily sending out clear and receptive energy.

THE RESCUER VIBER: This man comes to the rescue of many others, because he is kind and caring and uses rescuing to avoid dealing with the challenges of his own life. Like the Codependent Vibers, he feels good when saving others. Many men that slip into this vibe, may attract unbalanced women. The Rescuer thinks he can save others from despair. Quite often, the Rescuer Viber becomes resentful when he completes a rescue mission only to watch the now-healed woman leave him. As for the women, we are taught that some man will rescue us, so a certain amount of this vibe is comforting, as long as you keep it in balance.

THE SAD VIBER: This person shows visible pain in his eyes and in his body posture. In a low tone of voice, he carries old, sorrowful stories from his past into most conversations — draining others with the repetition. He has a heavyhearted energy.

THE SALESMAN VIBER: This pushy viber is always selling you something, especially himself. He tends to be polished and over-complimentary, and he definitely knows how to make others feel comfortable. Even when he is bossy, it's done in the most flattering way. He is a master salesperson, open and direct, constantly trying to close the deal on you (and he is the "deal"), so he will sell, sell, sell. He may say things like "*We would have soooo much fun together on my boat on the way to the* *islands! I'm taking you with me now!"* This vibe works on many women and don't be surprised if you attract women that expect you to treat them this way all the time. Will you be able to fulfill your promises? If so, it may be enough to sweep women off their feet! Beware: she may only want you for the vacation to the islands.

THE SEXUAL VIBER: This man sends out overpowering sexual signals that could knock women across the room. He drips with sexuality. He wants attention and knows how to get it. If you carry this energy, you can get attention with it, but unless sex is the goal, you may not get the long-term results you desire. On the receiving end, this sexual energy feels both flattering and intrusive, depending on the type of sexual vibes sent out. Sexual energy is the strongest energy on earth, and it can be transmitted in a pure or polluted form, depending on your thought behind it.

THE SHY VIBER: A quiet, kind, usually soft-spoken, introspective, slow starter with delicate energy. The Shy Viber is reserved and can come off seeming nervous and insecure in large groups and social situations.

THE SNOB VIBER: The snob is better than everyone, with an air of elitist arrogance. He usually doesn't connect with others because they are "below his standards." He won't give others the time of day and can make others feel "less than." The Snob Viber treats others with disrespect and can be sickening in the dating world, unless he's dating another snob. Just because he may have a higher social status or may be successful in his business life doesn't mean he is better than anyone else!

THE SPIRITUAL GURU/HEALER VIBER: A person that uses their intuitive psychic vibrations to heal, lead, and influence others using spiritual principles and connection to build trust. This vibration must be used with integrity and truth. Some people use this vibe to manipulate others with their power. Wrongly used, these actions can cause undue pain. If you are a healer, use your gift with honor and remember *what comes around goes around.*

THE TOUGH-GUY VIBER: This man looks like a tough guy on the outside and has a defensive look on his face. He sends out the vibes that he could punch your lights out if you say the wrong words. Inside and under this vibe is often a shy man that uses the tough-guy vibe to protect himself from rejection. He usually sits alone and is quiet until someone breaks through the shield of energy that protects him. Underneath this tough exterior is usually a sweetheart that has a lot to give.

THE VAMPIRE VIBER: Otherwise known as the Gas Guzzler. This is a needy and whiny man who worries, complains and sucks energy. He preys on the energy of other people. People feel exhausted after a Vampire Viber leaves their presence. Sometimes it feels like the life is sucked out of others when he is around. Just the sound of a Vampire Viber's voice can drain the energy in the room.

Now, after looking at the list, pick out the dominant energy vibes that you send out to the world. We send out these vibes with our thoughts, our eyes and in the tone and timber of our voice in conversations. I want you to look for different correlations in your experiences. In some cases, we attract the same type of vibration we put out. At other times, it's quite the opposite. We will avoid our type of vibes like the plague because we don't like the vibes a person sends out!

What about people you have dated or been married to? Can you figure out what vibe they sent out? (Of course, women have their own unique vibes too.) Can you see how important your vibes are in the attraction phase and in life?

If you have the courage to be honest with yourself, this is a place of awareness and power to shift from. Remember, your vibes affect others and vice versa.

The question we'll be answering is "*how do you change your vibes?*" Awareness is the first step! People grow through many levels of consciousness on their quest for fulfillment in life. As we grow and evolve, and put out our individual energy vibration, we will meet people that are on our same frequency. Are you satisfied with the people you have attracted into your life? Do you have the vibes that attract others into your life?

In the next chapter, I will show you how to work with your mind to shift into a higher vibration so you can attract people with a similar vibration. Remember that you are responsible for creating what you desire. Now we will explore the thoughts that create your life experiences and your energy.

Are you ready to see how easy it is to shift? Let's check your inner thoughts and get them in control...

INTERIOR CHECKLIST 3

"When you see a worthy person,

endeavor to emulate him.

When you see an unworthy person,

then examine your inner self."

--Confucius

ARE YOU DRIVING WITH CONFIDENCE?

HOW'S YOUR MENTAL ENGINE RUNNING, AND WHO'S STEERING YOUR THOUGHTS?

As I mentioned in Chapter 2, if you are open and you want to meet new people, you must first learn what vibe you send out and shift your energy and your internal states. That's what it takes — an open mental state and the internal work to back it up! If within the last year or two you've experienced rejections, lousy lovers, bad relationships or you have not been able to connect with the type of person you desire to be with, you may start to doubt yourself. You hear that inner voice — you know the voice that speaks to you and you can hear it again and again whispering in your ear, *"Maybe I'm not really that great. I want to find a mate, yet I don't know where to begin. No one wants me. Love is impossible to find. This is all too much effort."* You must get behind the wheel of your mind and steer those thoughts to correspond with your desired outcome.

As you think back on your last few interactions with women, how were you feeling? About yourself? About your appearance? About your worth? Did you leave the house tired and depressed to then have a bummer of an evening riddled with either negative people or none at all? Conversely, can you remember ever going out in one of your negative moods to find your friends all happy and ready to rock-n-roll — so that your energies didn't match all evening? Can you recall getting irritated because they were having a great time, and you felt invisible? Maybe you wanted to go home and wake-up on the other side of the bed, hoping you would snap out of your mood? You ask yourself *"How can I change this pattern?"*

You've already begun this exploration, so let's move toward achieving your goals and give you the tools to recreate your life from the inside out. You asked for the answer and now it's time to take action!

You could learn every line in this book, and then go anywhere in the world, and still, you will not meet *"the one"* unless your attitude and your energy equal what you are looking for. You must adjust your consciousness first, not just use techniques for flirting. What you say to yourself on a regular basis affects your results! Your confidence can get a little tweaked when you're new at something or haven't had much success in the past. You must re-tune your mind and stay focused in the same way you would if you were learning to play golf, to trade stock, or to master the computer. Take it step by step, be willing to risk, and you will learn how to create dynamic energy and build solid relationships. I guarantee it!

YOU ARE IN CONTROL OF YOUR VEHICLE AT ALL TIMES!

You are in control, and the control begins with your mental state and what you say to yourself daily. What do you say to yourself about your single status before going out into the world every-day? What are your thoughts before attending an event, a party or a meeting? Do you say *"God; I'm 35 and still alone!"* Or do you find yourself thinking *"It'll never happen for me...I'll never meet that special someone."* How about, *"All the good women are married or already taken. I hate being single. Its no use, no one wants me any way. I'm too old, too boring, too..."* whatever you continuously say in your mind.

Are you afraid that you're not good-looking enough, thin enough, in shape, smart, tall enough, or that you don't make enough money?

I can't be too emphatic about this: *WHAT YOU THINK DE-TERMINES WHAT YOU GET!* Your thoughts are the projector in your movie, and your movie is an outpicturing of your thoughts. Only you know what you are saying to yourself every day. You know how you feel about your body, your level of intelligence and about your personality. Are you constantly criticizing yourself casually in conversations? Because if you are, you will keep women away, and any woman who breaks through your judgment barrier will have the same judgments about you that you do. You can count on it!

If you want your dreams to come true, you must think only about what you wish to experience. This is the time to take back the control and steer your mind toward the outcome — not the problems or negative thoughts you carry around inside. We all have them and this internal diagnostic tuning will help you discover your prominent beliefs about love, yourself and the messages you send.

Your internal thoughts are the stepping-stones to your success. Who's in control of those thoughts anyway? *YOU ARE IN CONTROL OF YOUR MIND AT ALL TIMES!* Are you achieving your desired results with your current thoughts?

If not, then begin now to take back control! Say to yourself: *"I am embarking on a new plan. Something great is coming my way. Things are changing. I am open to new experiences that enhance my life now."* Realize you will always attract into your life what is in your mind. You are that powerful, and through this power you are attracting circumstances that lead you toward success or away from it. Again, I stress, to get your desired outcome, you must first open yourself up and believe that you deserve it.

When you hear *"I deserve love,"* what thoughts come into your mind? Do you believe you deserve love? Your body and mind will respond to your answer to those questions. Do you slump over, feeling down, or stand tall saying, *"Yes, I deserve love for sure."* Your thoughts affect your neurology, which influences your energy vibration and, finally, your results. Powerful information here!

Once again…you are in control of your vehicle at all times!

For example, you're walking into your office in a depressed mental state entertaining negative self-talk: *"I'm really lonely"* or *"I really don't have anything to offer anyone. I don't have anywhere to go to meet new people"*, or *"Oh, poor me, my woman just left me, and I'm ruined"*, or *"The last four dates have bombed so I give up"*, or *"I have the worst luck with women and I'm a loser."* How do you think these words affect your body language? This silent language is how you are presenting yourself to the world. Your body language follows your thoughts. Plenty of people get depressed when they're lonely, and their depression expresses itself in low energy levels and negative attitudes. What are your prominent thoughts right now about dating and deserving love? Are you aware of your invisible body language signals?

Imagine for a moment how much energy just one negative thought creates. Like a computer virus, it determines how you respond at a cellular level. It spreads to your body movements, it influences the way you walk and talk. That one negative thought becomes a self-fulfilling prophecy. These thoughts keep creating our circumstances and we get to keep being "right" about our lives.

The way you feel inside — and of course, the way you look on the outside — has an enormous impact on the energy flow between you and the people in your life. Especially women. Are you repelling or attracting right now? If you find yourself repelling, go into a higher gear, up-level your thinking. Repeat in your mind, *"I am open to meeting new people, and I'm attracting new experiences now! I have success with people, especially women!"* Your unconscious mind hears this and will respond accordingly. This powerful internal mechanic takes directions and follows our command. Are you commanding your thoughts powerfully, getting the results in your life now?

If you see a woman and think, *"I really want to meet her"*, and then you don't feel significant or confident enough to go over to her, how will she end up with you? You have to take risks without expectations. Do it for the adventure and the experience. You create your life every day. You are responsible! She is only one woman out of millions of available women. Risk it and know that one of these times the magic will happen, and you will succeed. Program that in your mind! *"I am willing to risk and I enjoy the process. I will succeed!"*

Take new risks, say something just for the fun of it and enjoy the moment without high expectations. Who knows? You might make a connection. Even if you don't, know that it will happen soon enough if you have the right attitude and use your thoughts powerfully.

The things you say to yourself right off the bat affect the confidence and joy level of your day. Do you wake up in the morning and think, *"Oh God, not another day! My life is so dead and boring!"* If you're unexcited about going to work because it's the same old thing, then you'll just be dragging around, and nobody will want to meet you in that state. You have to get yourself psyched up on a daily basis...and then be aware of what you say and of the energy you project in your words when you connect with others.

I was involved with producing a video called "Hot Tips on Dating Beautiful Women." As a result of extensive interviewing, we found that most women prefer a man with confidence. Physical good looks weren't all that necessary. Unlike most men, the good news is that women are not always after looks when it comes to their ideal mate. Women experience the world more through their ears, where men are more visual in nature. According to studies, for a man, looks are almost always in the top three desired qualities. Men want a good-looking woman. Historically, men are visually stimulated. A man will see a woman and just know she is "it". Of course, "it" is totally dependent on the picture he has in his mind of what is "perfect" for him. His childhood images and experiences create that picture, and sometimes it isn't realistic. Men act on impulse and sexual stimulus.

A close friend of mine is only attracted to women who look like Bridget Bardot/Pamela Sue Anderson. This corresponds with the visual that goes all the way back to when he was a five year-old. He has it set in his mind that a blonde with huge breasts is the only type for him for the long haul. As you can imagine, this considerably limits the women he connects with. I suggested that he open his options and experience all the unlimited possibilities.

For most women, "good looks" is anywhere between the fifth and the tenth most desired quality according to the surveys I have conducted. The most important traits to women are personality, honesty, integrity, values and financial stability. Many of these qualities are communicated to us in the first conversation we have with a man. We can hear it in your voice and see it in your body language. Women are automatically programmed to look for a stable and confident mate. We want a man who enjoys his career, because this makes us feel safer. "Security" is as important to women as "looks" are to men — although (let's be honest here) being "put together" can also be very helpful. It all begins with the first conversation.

So what is confidence? Confidence is feeling good about yourself and having self-assurance when you leave your house. The dictionary definition is: *To confide is to trust; boldness, assurance; intimacy.* This trust begins with yourself. The inner work you will do in this chapter is the first key to building your confidence and trusting your own internal voice to let you know what beliefs and thoughts are running you. That's right, from now on your life will be different as you take control of your thoughts and the words you use to describe yourself!

Until now in our society, men have been trained to be good

providers and to learn a skill to assist them to rise to the top, make big money to impress women and other men (with toys and accomplishments). Conversely, it has been accepted that women are more self-sufficent these days, emotionally open and are able to express deep feelings more easily than most men. Today, women expect men to be confident, emotionally available and conscious of what makes us happy. That means you need to, first, be fulfilled inside. Men want to make women happy and proud, so it's time to go a little deeper and get connected with your real beliefs and desires.

Some women expect that you have already done this deeper inner work and get disappointed when you don't seem together inside and out! Remember: most women have been trained to believe that you have all the answers and are going to be "The Prince" we were promised in fairy tales. We have many books that take us through simular processes and now you will be ahead of the game by doing this work! Believe me, there are many women that need this inner work and I'm currently writing the book for women.

THE FIRST IMPACT

Your inner beliefs about yourself come out in your initial conversations with women, which send out the first signal for connection. If your internal conversation is negative, you may lose the contact unless the woman is on the same negative vibration. Many men in private coaching sessions say they felt instant chemistry with a woman at an event but after talking with her she seemed distant or uninterested. What went wrong? I usually ask what they talked about and after role-playing, I quickly discover why she exited the scene. During the first conversation, many of us communicate unconsciously. If we were really aware of what we said and the vibes we sent out, we would know why women left after a few minutes. This is why I am inviting you to answer these questions to discover your automatic responses that may be turning women off. The truth is, women qualify men in the first five minutes with subtle questions that we have been trained to ask from many books and magazines.

Depending on which phase a woman is in, she will ask a few questions to see how you might match up. I had a man tell me up front that he loves to date many women and doesn't think he'll ever settle down and then wanted to be intimate with me on a first date. I mentioned that I had heard what he said earlier in the evening and that I wasn't interested in a casual sexual relationship and he responded, *"What made you think that's what I want?"* He was completely clueless about the impression he made earlier.

Too many men erroneously believe that if they expose all of their successes up front, it will capture a woman. *"I own a big company, an expensive car, a great condo."* It might work for some men who believe that this is all they have to offer, yet often the results are temporary. I have heard stories of men that have approached my female clients with lines like *"You look like a high maintenance woman and I have the cars, the house and the money you want!"* What a turn off! More often than not, they end up wondering why they were taken advantage of. What works more often is a feeling of self-assurance which shows in the way he communicates (i.e., his voice and the way he walks) and the energy vibe that he sends out.

Your voice is a powerful tool, and if it exudes confidence it makes you more appealing to a woman right from the start. In other words, the sound of your vehicle can make or break the deal. Women also want to be heard. Listening and remembering are vital, and what she says is key to discovering if you are on the same wavelength.

How do you create a winning impact right from the start? Your voice is a vital key in the attraction phase. Psychologist Don Gabor found in a study on the art of conversation that thirty-eight percent of powerful communication is based on the tone of your voice. Women are very aware of the texture of your voice. That is the first signal of the vibe you send. Fifty-five percent of successful communication is based on visual appearance and body language. Only seven percent of powerful communication is based on the words we speak.

Where do you fit in here? Do you sound shy, nervous, arrogant…or together? Practice saying "*hello*" with confidence and enthusiasm. Do you sound authentic? Nerdy? Nervous? Boring?

Have you ever walked into a room — a bar, an office — and you can just feel another man's energy, you can sense a presence without hearing a word out of his mouth and you wonder *Where does he get that dynamic charisma?* (Which means spirit). When he does speak, his voice sends out a frequency that makes you wonder, *What was it about him? He is so articulate and focused! What does he have that I don't?* You want to create the same dynamic energy about yourself. You want to make an impression that matches your desired results, right? This is the mental state I was speaking about earlier -- it begins with your consciousness and your inner beliefs about yourself, love and your life! It starts with what you say to yourself before you leave the house.

In my private coaching sessions, I uncover my clients' true mental state and help them shift those by using the questions you will answer later in this chapter. All of us have negative programs playing in our heads that we aren't even aware of: programs that run us on a daily basis. We have our higher self and our lower self and they both rear their heads at different times in our lives. We all know the difference when our lower self takes over, because it causes us to send out negative vibes and we feel disempowered. When we send mixed signals, we get mixed results, and it is caused by not being congruent with our thoughts and beliefs.

Part of the problem is not being clear or conscious of our internal thought processes, our goals and core beliefs that run us. This exercise will wake you up to yourself. You'll hear how you sound and how you say things, and you'll get a better idea of what kind of energy you put out and why you're not having success in certain areas of your life. You should notice a distinct shift in conscious awareness after doing this work. This is your unique internal diagnostic tune-up! This powerful exercise (on pages 72-80) takes time and focus, and the results are worth it!

You will understand what unconscious messages you send out without even knowing it. Then you can rebuild from there. The subconscious mind takes your words personally and literally, as do most people. When you combine powerful words with powerful emotions, your mind believes it and will create that belief in your experience. Being unconscious in your languaging prevents you from having loving relationships and creates energy-draining states that affect your vocal tone.

By focusing on your desired outcome and speaking with conviction and intention, you master your mind, upgrade your conversations and create your ultimate destiny. Think only about the results you want, reaffirming these to yourself periodically.

Remember, the beliefs and thoughts come first — followed by your words — and then your tone. You might not be able to see this in yourself, but think about the last person you talked to who had a droning or monotone voice. Borrrrrring! Or how about that teacher who put you to sleep?

Are you a drone? Your tone of voice, in combination with power words, becomes a direct vibration to others. If you want to change your life, from this moment on, become 100 percent aware of your words and the tone you use to communicate those words.

If your thoughts are negative or fearful, the words that come out of your mouth will be the same, and the tonality will match. The energy of negative or fear-based words can drain listeners and become downright repulsive for most people.

Think about it, people get to know you from what you tell them about yourself and from your tonal energy. Be careful what you tell others about yourself, because it could be repeated, especially if you spoke during a time of weakness; your message might not be what you want out in the world.

If you're sad, angry, or bitter and keep talking about your ex, your terrible divorce and your abject loneliness, this is what people think about you. Moreover, besides pushing others away, the emotions behind your negative words affect the cells and weaken your health. If you have to share, tell your sad stories to trusted friends who will not pass them on — polluted with their own opinions.

Here are a few checkpoints: Are your conversations leaving others with the thoughts you want them to have of you? People only remember what you tell them, and they will pass those words on (with their own interpretation mixed in) to others. Check out people who are around you right now. Do they represent how you feel about yourself? Every person you attract is a clear mirror of who you are in consciousness. Do you often think to yourself that there are no available people and have friends that don't show up for you? Do the people in your life represent what you truly deserve or desire? If not, take a deeper look within. You only receive what you believe you deserve! This is where NLP and other mind-shifting techniques come into play, because our subconscious mind attracts experiences to us according to our beliefs. Our subconscious mind:

- Takes our language literally
- Responds to feelings
- Runs our body
- Is always alert and functioning
- Receives directions from our conscious mind
- Responds to repetition
- Plays back what it receives in our life like a computer
- Takes everything personally

Now it's your turn to discover what comes out of your mouth and how you may be coming across to others! The Internal Diagnostic Tune-up is next. It will help you become more aware of the phases you're in and the vibes you send out. From now on, you'll learn to listen more intently to your inner dialogue before you speak.

Use the following exercise to find out both the thoughts and the energy behind your conversations and those of people you meet daily. The Internal Diagnostic Tune-up will assist you in figuring out what you talk about when you are out connecting with new people or hanging with your friends. Most of us talk unconsciously and would be surprised at what we say in casual conversations that affect the way we are perceived.

Let's take a look at your beliefs that contribute to your conversations and see how using powerful words can assist you in creating what you want every day.

SELF-TALK
THE INTERNAL DIAGNOSTIC TUNE-UP

It is very important to do this inner work and tune up the inner thoughts that run your life. You may want to write your answers in your journal, but it is preferable to say them aloud into a tape recorder. Even better, turn on a tape recorder and let a close friend ask you the questions. I think this helps bring out more of the real you, especially if you are an auditory person and can express yourself better with words.

Let the answers flow, so that you will become aware of the beliefs you have about yourself and get in contact with that inner voice that talks to you on a regular basis. You will also become aware of the messages that you unconsciously tell others if you examine your thoughts closely. In my seminars, I will often ask participants what kind of men they believe themselves to be and why they would be great partners. Invariably, half the audience gets tongue-tied. If you don't know why you're a good catch, how can you expect women to believe you are? You are the vehicle and you are revealing and selling yourself on a daily basis!

The Internal Diagnostic Tune-Up will help you become aware of the energy you project about yourself. For most men, this exercise is a real wake-up call!

So, be honest with your answers; come forth with your real thoughts, your true values, your underlying beliefs and your current goals. As you listen back, you'll uncover the content of your consciousness in your answers and your tone of voice.

We'll start with a series of belief questions. Again, you can write your answers in a journal, but using a recorder offers added insight and reflection while taping answers with a friend. If this isn't possible, you can ask yourself the questions and tape your responses. This taping session allows you to investigate how you sound and notice what energy your voice puts out. If you don't have a recorder, borrow one. This way, you'll become more aware of the image you project in your daily life by hearing yourself and your answers. Before doing this exercise, set up your environment: turn off your phone, pager, cell phone, and anything else that could distract you. If you have pets, feed them and put them in another room. If you have children put them to bed or down for a nap. Make this a priority and bring any items you need into the room (water, snacks, a journal, nice music).

Nobody's keeping score, so don't bother planning your answers — just let them flow out naturally and be as accurate and descriptive as possible. This is the deep, internal tuning that will show you the areas to strengthen and tune-up. Be excited, this is a way to get back the control of your life and win at love!

You'll notice that some of the questions may seem repetitive. This is designed to probe deeper into the unconscious mind and uncover the core beliefs that run our lives. Beliefs are a multilayered phenomenon. Sometimes, more than one combination of questions is needed to unlock the unconscious thought patterns.

First, you will gain the awareness of your core beliefs and then you will learn how to shift gears in order to head in the right direction for more success in all areas of your life with techniques that are simple to learn. Just let the answers come out naturally and be real with yourself.

Some of the questions may make you feel uncomfortable. This is a clear signal guiding you to issues that may need further tuning. You will be investigating your inner conflicts and shift them to be congruent with your future goals. The subconscious and unconscious mind takes these beliefs literally, and mixed beliefs will then create mixed results. By being really honest and answering from your gut, you will then uncover the basic core beliefs that are the cause of your current situation. No one (except your friend asking the questions) will be reading or listening to your answers, so explore deeper.

For Example: What is your core belief about still being single?

An answer might be something like this… *"I never thought I'd be this age and still be single. Sometimes I feel so alone and desperate and want love so badly I can't think straight."* Another answer might be " *Well it's been my choice up until now. I can honestly say I'm ready for love in my life!"* Get the picture? Just be honest and let the answers flow - then you'll see how your mind and thoughts have become your reality. If a question doesn't relate just skip it and move on.

WHAT ARE YOUR INNER THOUGHTS, CORE BELIEFS
AND COMMENTS THAT YOU MAKE TO OTHERS
ABOUT:

- *Living alone?*
- *Still being single?*
- *Being newly single?*
- *Growing in love with someone?*
- *Committing to a full-time relationship?*
- *Getting married?*
- *Being faithful?*
- *Having children?*
- *Your family?*
- *Activities you have the most passion for?*
- *Important people in your life?*
- *God? A Higher Power?*
- *Religious compatibility in relationships?*
- *Casual sex?*
- *Being friends first?*
- *Close, intimate friendships?*
- *A support system?*
- *Love?*
- *Relationships?*
- *Women?*
- *What makes you a good choice to date?*
- *Why you would make a good partner?*
- *Where you see yourself in 2 years?...5 years?...10 years?*
- *The seven most important qualities and values you must have in a relationship?*

- ◆ What you have to offer a mate?
- ◆ Your best qualities?
- ◆ Areas in your life that need tuning?
- ◆ Values in relationships?
- ◆ The values that are most important to you in life?
- ◆ Your physical appearance?
- ◆ What is most important to you in life?
- ◆ Your strengths of character?
- ◆ Being in love? Do you enjoy being in a relationship?
- ◆ Being ready or open to love?
- ◆ Romance?
- ◆ The qualities of a desirable woman? Do you have those qualities?
- ◆ The energy you currently project?
- ◆ Your fears of loneliness?

RATE THE LEVEL OF SATISFACTION IN YOUR LIFE NOW FROM 1-10 (1 BEING LOWEST -10 BEING HIGHEST)

- ◆ How satisfied are you with your current home environment? _____
- ◆ How satisfied are you with your work environment? _____
- ◆ How fulfilled are you with the work you do? _____
- ◆ How satisfied are you with your personal/social life? _____
- ◆ How satisfied are you about how you treat yourself? _____
- ◆ How satisfied are you with your financial situation? ___
- ◆ How satisfied are you with your spiritual and religious practices? _____
- ◆ How satisfied are you with your vacations/play time? _____ With male friends? _____ or with a partner? _____
- ◆ How satisfied are you with your spare-time activities/hobbies? _____
- ◆ How satisfied are you with your current social network and friends you hang with? _____
- ◆ How satisfied are you with your fitness regime? _____ Eating habits? _____
- ◆ How satisfied are you with your appearance? _____
- ◆ How satisfied are you with your alone-time? _____
- ◆ How satisfied are you with your family life? _____

Review your answers to the previous questions. Pick out the satisfying — and the not-so-satisfying — situations in your life. This will help you become more fully aware of how you're coming across to others. (Once you are cognizant, your energy-draining words can be replaced.) The numbers you chose will indicate the areas to focus on in your inner tune-up. Any numbers below six can be considered a tune-up spot.

More Questions

- *How would you describe yourself in ten words?*
- *What is your favorite saying?*
- *Are you ready to love someone?*
- *What attracts you first when you meet a woman?*
- *What attributes must she have to keep you attracted?*
- *What does the word "commitment" mean to you?*
- *Do you desire commitment?*
- *Can you be committed? Do you want to be committed now?*
- *Are you afraid to trust someone with your heart?*
- *What are you afraid would happen if you did?*
- *What are the reasons you would want to commit? Or not??*
- *What would the experience of being in love be like to you?*
- *Can you imagine your life with someone great who adores you? How would you describe it?*
- *Do you want to have love in your life now?*
- *How do you picture love?*
- *Do you think you deserve love?*
- *Did you have any strong role models in relationships?*
- *What is so powerful in these role-model relationships that you would like to create for yourself?*
- *Are you worthy of what you're asking for?*
- *What is most important to you in your life?*
- *Do you have good energy?*
- *Are you sensitive to other people's energy?*
- *Do you have a support system in your life now?*
- *Are you willing to ask for support?*
- *What are your strengths?*
- *What are your weaknesses?*

- Are you a man of your word?
- Do you keep your word to yourself?
- How important is being on time to you?
- Are you an open communicator when things get rocky in friendships or relationships?
- What are your best qualities?
- What are your best physical attributes?
- What area of your life needs your attention now?
- Are you a good communicator?
- What are some of the things that turn you on to a person?
- What irritates you in a person you date?
- Are you a good listener?
- How do you enjoy receiving love? By feeling it, seeing it, talking about it?
- What excites you about being in a relationship?
- What scares you about a relationship?
- Are you open-minded about lovemaking/ sex?
- Do you have any sexual hang-ups?
- What are the qualities that make you who you are?
- Are you ready to receive love? Give love?
- Are you afraid that love might not happen for you?
- Do you have any commitment issues that you're aware of?
- What is love to you and is it important for you to have in your life?
- What is your ultimate goal in life?
- Do you have a life mission?
- Where did your beliefs come from?
- Are you willing to shift gears on some of the beliefs running you?

The next set of questions deals with dates and meeting people. Ask these questions of yourself first — or let a friend do the questioning. After you have worked on your own answers, you should be more aware of how you sound and the vibe you send out. Then you will start to hear the messages and feel the energy in other people's conversations. When you ask questions of others, listen for the value words in the answers, and become aware of their primary communication style (explained in chapter 10). The more you do this, the easier it is to learn about the people in your life. Asking a woman questions to find out her interests puts you in the driver's seat and saves time, because you'll be able to figure out her phase and her vibrational energy and know if you want her in your life.

These more personal questions are appropriate for meeting people as they quickly uncover one's values and passions. When you ask these questions of a prospective connection, listen to the key words in her answers. Depending on your top values and the phase you're interested in exploring, you can determine if this relationship will fulfill your desired outcome. You can ask these questions intermittently during dates or when just meeting people. Don't bring out the list and ask them directly. Be subtle and listen closely to what people say. You will become a powerful communicator by listening and being in tune with the words that are used when someone is answering you. You'll become a good conversationalist by asking questions and being an observant and interested listener.

QUESTIONS TO ASK AND ANSWER TO DISCOVER MORE ABOUT YOURSELF AND PROSPECTIVE PARTNERS:

- *What excites you about life? What are you passionate about?*
- *When you have time off, what is your favorite thing to do?*
- *Where is your ideal place to "chill out"?*
- *Do you enjoy your chosen profession and why?*
- *What makes you happy? Brings you the most joy in your life?*
- *If you could be anything you wanted, what would it be?*
- *When you were younger, what did you want to be when you grew up?*
- *Are you active? What is your favorite physical activity?*
- *What are the top seven values that you possess in life?*
- *Tell me about your family/heritage?*
- *What is your definition of a good relationship? Intimacy?*
- *What were you like as a child? What was your childhood like?*
- *Are you fond of traditions? Do you have any that you created?*
- *Does your family have any unique traditions?*
- *If you could create a new tradition for yourself, what would it be?*

- Tell me about your mother and father?
- Do you have any mentors or role models in life?
- What is your biggest life accomplishment to date?
- Find five adjectives that describe you mentally to others? Physically?
- What has been your most exciting vacation and why?
- What are the values you are seeking in a mate?
- What is your religious background?
- Do you go to church regularly? Is that an important part of your life?
- Do you have to have a spiritual partner?
- What are your spiritual practices?
- What music gives you goose bumps? Top three favorites?
- What is your favorite food/restaurant?
- Do you have a favorite saying?
- What is your favorite language? Do you speak more than one?
- What is your favorite holiday?
- What is your favorite dessert? Where do you like to get it?
- Do you like to dance? What music do you like to dance to?
- If you had all the money in the world, what would you do with it?
- What are your favorite types of vacations, and where have you traveled?
- If you could have any wish, what would it be?
- Where do you see yourself in one year? Two years? Five years?
- What is your favorite story that you like to tell at parties?
- What did you like to dress up as for Halloween? Did you like Halloween as a child?
- What were you like as a child? Where did you grow up?
- What were some of your favorite TV shows as a child?
- Who is your favorite actor or film star?
- What is your favorite movie?
- What are your favorite albums from the 50s, 60s, 70s, 80s, 90s and now?
- What were you like in high school?
- What did you enjoy studying?
- Did you have a high school sweetheart?

- *Have you ever been in love?*
- *Who was the love of your life?*
- *What qualities made her special?*
- *What was your longest relationship?*
- *Why didn't you marry? Or, if you did what caused the separation/divorce?*
- *Did you have animals growing up?*
- *What animal would you use to describe yourself?*
- *Who are the most important people in your life now?*
- *What accomplishment are you most proud of?*
- *What is a secret you've never told anyone about yourself?*
- *What things (activities, items, food, etc.) make you smile?*
- *Do you have any fetishes? Name one.*
- *What is your ideal, romantic date?*
- *What is your relationship to money? Do you enjoy it or worry about it?*
- *Do you like children? Have any? Want any?*
- *Have you ever dated a woman with children?*
- *What makes you worth knowing?*
- *Who is your best friend? What makes him/her so special?*
- *How do you handle the stresses of life?*
- *How do you feel about drinking and drugs?*

By answering these questions and listening to your own responses, you will realize the energy that you send out with your words. You also may have discovered some topics and subjects that you hadn't thought of before and how you view life. By asking these questions you're getting in touch with the deeper side of yourself. Isn't it revealing to get to know yourself?

You can use your responses to create your ideal relationship list and utilize these answers on the Internet if you're into on-line dating. Remember, online you're being asked questions all the time, and the words you use in your answers are the initial connection. Online dating is one of the latest and most amazing ways to connect for the busy person, so be aware of the message you send! The written description you send is the first "energy" that a person receives from you. In the next chapter is a list of adjectives you can use to describe yourself and your ideal mate for writing ads on-line and for the personals.

I help thousands of people write out the profiles that will impact the people that they are connecting with online. Words are powerful… use them wisely online and in person. Use your answers from above questions to create powerful answers online and to write your goals in love. I suggest writing these qualities out and keep revising your list as you grow, and you will see this woman manifest in your life. First ask yourself: *"Are you what you are asking for?"*

When asking these questions, you will uncover the values that are important to others – if you're listening. Many women who have read this book have confided that secretly they wanted to ask men the questions that follow. After getting to know someone, you may want to discuss some of these subjects openly. Sex and intimacy are important to women, and we want to feel connected to a man before we can open up in the intimacy area. Since so many people are having sexual connections prior to marriage it is important to discuss deeper issues.

Asking these questions and discussing topics to get clear on your values about sex and intimacy and what they mean to you is vital. We all have different core beliefs, and it is important to discuss your thoughts and beliefs and not assume you know what someone thinks. When dating partners have intercourse it tends to change the dynamics of the relationship depending on the people involved. Having intercourse may carry a different meaning to a woman than it does to a man. I suggest that you discuss this topic before you shift into the intercourse gear. Without clear communication first, sometimes expectations can create tension and heartbreak. If a woman asks you, tell her the truth. Don't pretend or lie to get what you want.

QUESTIONS WOMEN REALLY WANT
TO ASK YOU BUT RARELY DO

- *Does having sex make you feel committed to a woman?*
- *Should a woman wait until you commit before giving you the gift of herself sexually?*
- *Are you looking for a real relationship?*
- *What makes you decide it's the right time to connect deeper?*
- *What makes you grow in love with a woman?*
- *Is it important for you to keep your promises? Are you a man of your word?*
- *What is your distinction between making love and having sex?*
- *What are your thoughts on being monogamous? Are you capable of being monogamous?*
- *Do you respect a woman that desires to wait until after marriage to make love?*
- *Will you think I'm easy if we make love too soon? What is your definition of too soon?*
- *What are your thoughts on dating a powerful woman?*
- *What is your description of an attentive lover?*
- *Do you have hang-ups about sex? What are they?*
- *Is kissing important to you? What makes someone a good kisser?*
- *How willing are you to take responsibility for contraception?*
- *Are you a commitment-oriented man or commitment-phobic?*
- *How important is sex to you in a relationship?*
- *Do you believe in foreplay? Describe your version of foreplay.*
- *Are you paying all this attention to me because you like me or because you are needy or just want to conquer me?*
- *What are your fantasies?*
- *Are you into porno? Sex toys? Swapping? If so, how often?*
- *How often do you enjoy having sex? Are you a morning, daytime or evening lover?*
- *What do you like about my body?*
- *What about me attracted you?*
- *How do you feel when a woman calls you or asks you out?*
- *What in your mind makes you consider marrying a woman?*
- *What will you do if I fall in love with you?*
- *Will I hear from you after we make love?*

Many of these questions are intense and take some thought and time to answer. This work will assist you in becoming more clear in your communication with women and all people in your life. Because of the various topics covered in this chapter, I encourage you to come back and do this important exercise. This is the key to breaking your patterns and creating a new life! You must know yourself first!

Now that you are aware of what you are thinking internally, next on our tune-up list is your unique sound effect. Let's explore how you sound and what you tell others about yourself in conversations about your life...

YOUR UNIQUE
SOUND EFFECT

*"What kills a skunk is
the publicity it gives itself!"*

--Abraham Lincoln

Now that you answered the questions from the last chapter into a tape recorder, you are undoubtedly becoming more aware of the tone and the words that automatically come out of your mouth in conversations (and the thoughts that created them). It's an eye-opener to finally realize your energy mode in delivering your answers and the messages they reveal.

So, how does your voice sound — resonance, tone and the vibration — when you are speaking? Are you descriptive or boring? Are you interesting to listen to? Do you use words that send out different signals than what you thought you were sending? Are you aware of the vibration and deeper beliefs about love that come out of your mouth? The inner tune-up takes consistency and conscious awareness to create new conversation skills and to establish stronger, more supportive belief patterns.

Since our words create impressions that others have of us, it's empowering to know we can now control our thoughts and words. Here are actual quotes I've heard from people in social situations. After reading these words, you will see why some people are still alone.

83

CONVERSATIONS AND COMMENTS THAT CREATE NEGATIVITY:

♦ *I should go out, but I'm tired (it is too far, I don't want to go alone, I never meet anyone anyway...)*
♦ *I don't think love ever lasts.*
♦ *I'll be happy when I meet someone /lose weight/ work out/ clean my place/ feel great/ look for a new job.*
♦ *Love hurts!*
♦ *You can't trust women!*
♦ *Women don't like me.*
♦ *I'm too lazy/ insecure/ hurt/ tired or broke to meet women.*
♦ *Maybe someday I will look, but I'm too scared/ too shy/ too unavailable/ brokenhearted/ fed up/ afraid of rejection...*
♦ *Love is impossible to find. I'll try again someday.*
♦ *This party stinks. I never connect with anyone.*
♦ *I hate going to these events -- they are sooo boring.*
♦ *I always meet jerks at places like this.*
♦ *Everyone is so unattainable when I go out.*
♦ *I can't find a good woman/girlfriend.*
♦ *I never meet anyone. I never will.*
♦ *Women are difficult. They only want men with cash!*
♦ *I don't like dating. Why bother.*
♦ *It's hard to find someone at these events.*
♦ *I always give and get nothing in return.*
♦ *I'm not good enough to meet her.*
♦ *I need a date. I'm so depressed.*
♦ *I hope I will find someone, but I doubt I will. I give up!*
♦ *I can't imagine someone loving me.*
♦ *I'm sure I won't connect, because I'm too fat/ too broke/ too ugly/ too depressed.*
♦ *It's impossible for me to meet anyone!*
♦ *These people are losers.*

Do any of these sound familiar? It all begins with those nasty old thoughts, and now that we are aware of them, we can recognize how they tend to pollute our conversations. Again, if you haven't done so already, I encourage you to answer the questions in the previous chapter into a tape recorder without trying in any way to edit yourself. Speak freely, then listen back to the tape and review your answers. You'll hear those automatic beliefs and the descriptive words that fly from your mind and out of your mouth. They creep into our mind like a virus. How much energy do these thoughts take up in your life and your body?

Single life can be challenging at times. Many singles have bouts of fear, anxiety, depression, sadness and anger and do talk about those challenges more often than not. We experience rejection, feel overwhelmed with responsibilities and confidence issues about single life. Know that as you tune into what you say, all of your beliefs will be shifting as you become more aware of your thoughts. Remember to work daily on your own negative thoughts as they arrive in your mind.

If you've experienced a few rejections, some lousy lovers, a handful of bad relationships, or other situations that have frustrated you, you may start to have doubts. You may say to yourself, *"Maybe I'm not really that great."* Remember, as you become more aware of what comes automatically out of your mouth, you will get better in conversations and become conscious of the energy you send out. There is no question about it!

Once you are aware, it is easy to change by giving some commands to your subconscious mind on a regular basis. After a short while, doing this becomes a habit and the results you experience will encourage you to do a repeat performance. Take the words and add the emotions and sensations you will feel when these experiences come into your life. *ACT AS IF* you have already experienced your goal and it will come! Take control!

The goal is clear: we want to let go of old beliefs and habits rather than drag them around with us. They drain our energy and bring us down, and they force us to recreate the same old life experiences and attract the same type of people and experiences over and over.

If you want to get better results, if you really want to meet someone different than in the past, raise the bar on your conversations. Using more positive sentence starters will change the way you are perceived — and begin to pave the way towards the life you want to create.

UP-LEVEL YOUR THOUGHTS AND CONVERSATIONS
(Here are a few examples. Add your own endings...)

♦ *I'm heading in the direction of...success in all areas of my life.*
♦ *I will...meet the perfect person for my life now!*
♦ *I'm clear that I am ready...to meet someone special!*
♦ *My clear intention is...to have a relationship that is an example to others.*
♦ *I'm committed to...having only the best for myself in all my relationships.*
♦ *I'm enthusiastic about...having an extraordinary relationship!*
♦ *I'm definitely focused on...achieving all my goals now!*
♦ *I am happy to report that...my life is going well and I'm sure I'll reach my goals!*
♦ *I choose to...recreate my inner thoughts.*
♦ *I desire...to have a relationship that works!*
♦ *My choice is...to be the love I'm am seeking!*
♦ *It is for sure that...I will connect with a great partner!*
♦ *I believe that...I deserve only the best for myself!*
♦ *I give meaning to...*
♦ *I have the vision for...*
♦ *I know for myself that...*
♦ *I can achieve...*
♦ *My highest choice is...*
♦ *I will surely create...*
♦ *My vision for my love life is...*
♦ *One of the unlimited possibilities is...*

Do you feel the difference in these statements? When you shift your words? By becoming clearer with your words, you will open up many new experiences and attract different people into your experience. Just try it. It works! Check the examples (in chapter 10) on energy producing thoughts and phrases.

ELIMINATE NEGATIVITY

How about what other people say to you about yourself? Many of us are powerfully influenced by others' opinions. Are you influenced by what others think of you? If you're honest with yourself, you will be shocked at how your mind is influenced by others' views. Again, their views and opinions are created from their deeper beliefs. What can you do in the moment when someone offers an opinion that just might slide some negativity into your mind?

Replace the negative belief in that moment with what you desire to feel and experience instead. If someone spews negative talk at you, say to yourself, *"No, I refuse to let this person's opinion and thoughts penetrate me."* If others say negative things to you in a conversation (in response to your new focus), just say to them (and yourself), *"That isn't true for me and I'd appreciate you keeping your opinions to yourself from now on, thank you."* Set boundaries! Then say inside your own mind, *"I dissolve that energy-draining thought and cancel it now! It is only an opinion and everybody's opinions are based on their own set of beliefs."*

How can you tell if a person influences you in a energy draining way? Check in with your inner voice, your center (where those gut feelings come from) and ask yourself these questions below to re-align your thoughts. Your body will signal (usually your stomach) and your intuition will give you the answer when you ask yourself the right questions. Listen to your gut… it knows. Look at the lives of those giving you their opinions.

To Re-Align, Ask Yourself:

♦ *Are the beliefs of this person what I desire to experience? Is this person's life one I'd like to lead? (If not, cancel that thought they just injected you with)*

♦ *Does this conversation, or these words, up-level my energy?*

♦ *How much energy is this conversation taking away or adding to me and my goals? (1 Lowest - 10 Highest)*

♦ *Is this amount of energy (negative or positive) helping to solve my challenges now?*

+ *Is their energy one you want to emanate?*
+ *What thought(s) would be the better choice right now?*
+ *Is this person supporting my life and growth?*
+ *Why should I take their beliefs so seriously?*
+ *Are these comments and opinions draining me?*
+ *What conversations/feelings/beliefs would be more beneficial now?*

Actually tell yourself out loud when negativity is heading your way: *"These words are not true for me"* (unless you are asking for constructive words from a therapist, coach or a friend you can trust*)*. At that time replace it with the new energy-producing thoughts or words. Then reflect on what and where their advice or opinion is coming from? Then let the other person know that you don't accept the beliefs about whatever subject they commented on. For example, a friend might say, *"You're a loser with women these days! Why not just give up on this game with women... They are impossible!"* You might say to him *"That is your opinion and it isn't true for me. I'm learning how those types of statements keep creating the same situations. Keep them to yourself from now on please."* Say to yourself (in that moment in your head), *"My mind is free from others' opinions. The doubt and fear are dissolved now. I know* (inject the new belief in the moment) *that I attract positive people in my life that appreciate me for who I am as a man. My higher self knows this new thought is true now!"* Erase his or her opinion in the moment. Do this until it becomes a habit and then rid yourself of those people who are not supporting you in your growth.

If this doesn't work, you may want to take a deeper look inside. Write out what is going on for you after being triggered by some else's opinion. What thoughts creep in? Write out what you believe you deserve – then observe the mind and the energy-draining chatter that comes to the surface. Are the comments you heard that disturbed you the truth? Use this feedback to deal with issues, not hide behind them. Perhaps this is an issue you may want to face and explore in a coaching session? Do some comments contain a grain of truth? Why does their opinion set you off balance?

Some comments trigger old memories, and you must realize that is an automatic response that you can change in the moment with techniques used by NLP (Neuro Linguistic Programming) practitioners. Those memories are stored in the subconscious and can reactivate emotions that cause you to trigger old emotions and intensify your current situation. Many times your feelings are triggered from stored memories. This reinforces your belief system, which creates your reality. This will occur over and over until the emotional charge is erased and reprogrammed for success.

Be aware: unsupportive people could attempt to sabotage you. If you know who those people might be, don't bother mentioning your vision or goals to them. Keep the vision to yourself! Hold the energy to do your inner work and don't disperse energy to those who suck it from you. It's a waste of words and energy trying to convince people that are negative. You will use your new found energy in better ways from now on. Just become the new you without talking about it to anyone who isn't on your side (or who drains your energy). Without saying a word, they will see the results in your life. Perhaps you will become an influential example to them in the future.

Take the time to pay closer attention to others. Slow yourself down to listen more intently to the people you meet. Go deeper inside, open up and sense if they would enhance your life or drain you. Don't bother to waste your energy on negative people from now on. Listen to your heart and gut feelings, and you'll find the intuitive sense about the people that surround you.

Focus on your deepest dreams and intentions and work on the negative *ENERGY-DRAINING* beliefs that creep into your mind that attempt to destroy *ENERGY-PRODUCING* beliefs. Once you do this regularly, then you can be sure that you'll desire to eliminate people that may be contributing to those beliefs. Remember: your life will be affected by what you say and hear in conversations, so keep your mind free of polluted, negative words and become an example for others to follow. Rid yourself of negativity and the people that add to conversations that bring you down.

Whatever you constantly think about is the issue that is calling for your attention. A huge shift will happen if you allow yourself to get to the root of the matter once and for all. Forgive yourself for allowing these beliefs to run you off the road and take control of your vehicle and your life. These are simple NLP techniques that assist you to erase old memories — then choose new beliefs. You're the master at the wheel. Move up to a new frequency.

SHARE YOUR VISIONS WISELY

It is vital to choose sacred people with whom to share your visions, dreams, challenges, secrets and fears. We make our choices with every word we utter or contemplate, and the friends we have around us reflect those choices. These friends, and the conversations we have with our support team, are a representation of our belief about what we deserve.

Be acutely aware of the powerful words that come out of your mouth when sharing your thoughts and visions with friends and family. These conversations and the words you use, will set the picture in their minds for success or failure for you. Are your conversations aligned with the results you desire? People feel it when you are clear and passionate about something or someone. The people you work with, socialize with and the things you tell people about yourself are all vital keys to creating a fulfilled life…Choose your friends and words carefully.

When people ask how you are, tell them that you're "*doing well, tuning yourself up, and making great changes in your life.*" Even if you're experiencing challenging times, just say you're focused on moving forward in new directions, creating new experiences for yourself and living life right now. Although you are being very vague, this is an effective technique to eliminate complaining and giving them an answer. If they ask for details, tell them the truth about your inner tuning. You may become a living example for them because you're changing old habits and working on new strategies for success.

Your friends may think you're crazy at first and they may not back you up because they aren't comfortable with you changing. You may discover that you might need to get some new road partners, because you will grow from this process and not feel as connected to their energy because you have changed. The most valuable action to take is to give them a copy of this book to have them do the work along with you. Pass it on! You then become the new role model for your friends and you may be the influential person to change their life forever! What an awesome feeling!

Now you will take this powerful knowledge and create the vision for your dream relationship...

ALIGN YOUR VISION 5

"If one advances confidently in the direction of his dreams, and endeavors to live the life which he has imagined, he will meet with success unexpected in common hours."

--Henry David Thoreau

GET CLEAR AND ALIGN YOUR VISION

Your next step in the process is becoming clear on what type of partner you want to create in your life in whatever phase you are in. What kind of woman do you desire to be with? Have you ever described your ideal mate? Do you ever share the vision of your ideal relationship with anyone? People spend years and years on marketing plans to create what they want in business and searching for the perfect car to drive, yet most of them never really think deeply about the type of person they want as a life partner. Let your imagination run free, and write your heart's desires down in detail. This is important for you to stretch yourself and go beyond your normal comfort zone and this is your chance to use your expanded thinking now. Use your imagination to align your vision and use the list of questions to direct you. After reading the questions, review the list of adjectives that you can use in your descriptions listed at the end of this chapter. If you hear your old negative programming attempting to leak into your writing, plug up those thoughts in the moment.

DESCRIBE YOUR IDEAL WOMAN IN DETAIL

PHYSICAL DESCRIPTION Since most men are so visually stimulated...What does your ideal woman look like? For example, is she the earthy type, the natural type, the business professional, the fashion model? Is she athletic, curvy, voluptuous, tanned and toned? What is her hair color and how does she wear her hair? How tall is she, how much does she weigh, what is her body type, etc...? Get descriptive!

CAREER CHOICE What does she do in her life? Do you want to be with a woman with a solid career, or with one who's going to stay home? Do you want a natural country girl, a homemaker/mother, or a woman who works part-time? How important is her financial independence to you?

EDUCATION LEVEL How important is her education level? Does she have to be on the same level as you? Are you worried that she may be more educated — or smarter —than you? If she is in school, is that okay with you?

PERSONALITY TYPE Does she have an open, extroverted, friendly personality? Is she a little more subdued, quiet and soft spoken? In between? How would you describe her personality? How does she act with you alone or in groups?

HOW DO YOU FEEL WHEN YOU'RE WITH YOUR MATE? Write this out in detail. For example, *"I feel so supported, nurtured, and creative in her presence. We can really open up and connect. She's so sweet and responsive, and she honors our relationship. I'm proud to have her in my life."*

COMMON ACTIVITIES What kinds of activities do you share with your woman? Do you want to create a relationship in which you're doing everything together or do you want more independence? If you're a busy man, do you want an equally busy woman, or when you come home, do you want the little woman waiting for you with pot roast? Some say, total opposites make the best couples and others disagree. It's your choice! Maybe you'd prefer that she work all day, so you can stay home and take care of the kids. How much interdependence — or dependence — are you looking for? You get to co-create the relationship you desire depending on what you want.

FAMILY You marry into a woman's family. What is your ideal family scenario? What if she is very close to her family and you aren't into the family scene? How would that play out? What if she detests your family? How important is this issue to you? Is this a deal-breaker for you?

SEX/INTIMACY Your beliefs around this issue are vital in a long-term relationship. When it comes to sex and intimacy, what kind of person do you want? Do you believe in sex before marriage? Are you into kissing, lovemaking, and sensuality? Answering the questions in the end of Chapter 3 will assist you in becoming clearer on this issue. Some people aren't sexual, and they meet somebody who is, who tries to teach them. Do you mind if a woman isn't experienced sexually? Are you in touch with your values on this issue? What if she has been sexually active? Do you judge a woman who is sexually experienced? Do you want a woman to tell you what she wants from you sexually? Are you open to learning how to please her? Have you studied the art of pleasing a woman sexually?

ROMANCE Is your woman romantic? What is your unique definition of romance? Describe a romantic evening with your ideal mate.

RELIGION Religious beliefs are very important in relationships, especially to people who are part of a specific religious culture. Your religious affiliation and your spiritual practices have a major affect on your relationships if religion is a value high on your list. Does your mate have to have the same religious background? Is religion a deal-breaker for you? Do you want to attend religious services and expect your mate to join you? Is prayer a part of your life? How about meditation or other practices? Are you not at all into religion and refuse to have a mate who is? If you are not on the same spiritual path, it is possible to be together if both parties discuss it openly? We all have the right to have our own beliefs, but if you want to pray and practice rituals of your religion and your mate isn't interested or supportive, it can cause problems in the future with your children and the families.

EATING HABITS Does your mate have to have similar eating habits? How important is this issue with you? Vegetarian? Meat eater? Healthy eater? Junk-food junkie? Describe your preference. Do special food restrictions bother you? Do you have any special food restrictions yourself? Are table manners important to you?

ALCOHOL AND MIND-ALTERING SUBSTANCES Does your mate drink, smoke marijuana, or use other drugs? Would it disturb you if your mate were on a prescription drug — such as Prozac or anti-depressants — to maintain mood balance? What if your mate was in a 12-step program? Does that matter to you? Do you think you should communicate about this before getting married?

MONEY Money issues and spending habits are a very important issue. Do you know how you will handle bills? Spending? Organizing and saving money? Would you be able to support a woman or feel comfortable with her having her own income? Do you want an equal partnership in the relationship where money and spending are concerned? Do you need a prenuptial agreement before you marry? Do financial challenges sway you from being interested in a woman long-term? Do you see yourself being the provider in the relationship? How does that feel to you in your day-to-day life? She doesn't work and you take care of it all, or she works and uses her earnings for certain expenses. What are those?

CHILDREN Do you like kids? Do you want your own? Do you

have a time-line in mind? Does a woman's time clock tick you off? Do you mind if she has children? Are you ready for the responsibility and financial realities of having children?

ANIMALS Are you an animal lover? If you're not, but she has animals, is that okay with you? If you're allergic, will that be an issue? If you love her, will you bend on this one?

SLEEPING HABITS If your mate is a night owl and you're an early morning riser, is this an issue? Does snoring bother you? Are you a heavy snoring machine? Are you a snuggler? Some people will say *"I want to be with a snuggler,"* and then others will say *"Oh God, I have to sleep by myself; I don't want anybody touching me when I sleep!"* Windows open or closed at night? Sleeping habits are adjustable yet we all have our unique sleeping habits?

PUBLIC BEHAVIOR How does she treat you in public? Does her energy change? Are you proud to be seen with her? Are you into being affectionate in public or private about PDA (public display of affection)? How do you want to be treated in public? How do you expect her to be when you're out with friends? Family? What are your expectations of how you should treat her?

FRIENDS Does she have nice friends? Describe them. How does she treat others? Do her friends like you? Do you enjoy her friends, or doesn't this matter to you? Are her friends a good reflection of her? Could you enjoy hanging out with them if they are a big part of her life? Does it matter if your friends like her? Will you be proud to introduce her to your friends?

HOBBIES What activities will you share? Is it important to have similar hobbies? If so, what would you enjoy sharing with your mate? Are you more into having separate interests? Do you want to have her around the boys?

COMMITMENT ISSUES Do you know how she feels about commitment? What she expects if you make love? What she is looking for in a committed relationship?

DAY-TO-DAY LIVING How will it be on a day-to-day basis? Describe a day in your life with your mate. What will it be like?

VALUES What are her strongest values? Which values are most important to you for her to possess? Do they have to match yours totally?

PARTNERSHIP What would make you happy in a partnership? What does "partner" mean to you in relation to your perfect match? What is your definition of a good partner?

PASSIONS What passions will you share? Describe them in detail.

It's very important to write your goals for your life and focus on the values and attributes that mean the most to you. Then you can speak clearly to others about your goals! Once you list your most important values, you can then ask questions that will let you know right away if there is a match in values with the women you meet. Those questions are in Chapter 3. Ask and listen to the answers carefully and save yourself time and energy if there isn't a match. You are clear on your intentions and communicate those intentions by knowing what you want first!

Another important key is to ask yourself , *"What would I be doing right now if the love of my life were here now? How would I be acting?"* In my classes, many people will say… *"When I'm in a relationship, then I'll …feel like cleaning my place, working out, taking a cooking class, buying a new couch, getting into theater, going to more concerts, taking better care of my car and my body."*… Get the picture? How will you treat yourself when you're in love? Do those things *NOW*! Be in harmony with the vibration you want to receive and it will show up! You have to do this with confidence and belief…

ACT AS IF!
BECOME WHAT YOU ARE ASKING FOR!

ALIGNMENT EXERCISE

After you have written out your unique goals, you can then easily program into your subconscious mind all the feelings that these descriptions represent to you. In order for you to attract a woman, you must first believe and conceive these goals as true! You must believe that you deserve a great relationship and are willing to receive it! Just like imagining your business succeeding, you create a clear picture in your mind of your ideal relationship succeeding now!

Before sleeping or while relaxing, consciously create in your body the sensations behind these descriptions of your ideal mate. Play soft, relaxing music and get relaxed. Use music that creates a romantic feeling inside you. Every time you hear this music it will anchor you into a state of being loved and connected.

Allow the feelings of being totally loved by a wonderful woman into your mind and body. Use your senses. How will she smell and feel in your arms? Where do you see yourself with her? What is the ambiance of the environment? The lighting? The scents? The sounds? The food? How does her skin feel against yours? What will she be saying to you about yourself? How will it feel making love to her? Massaging each other? Kissing? Eating together? How much joy surges through you while passionately connecting? Imagine how you will co-create an environment for your home, your vacations together, and enhance your life-style by being together. What is it like sharing a life of friends, family and spiritual practices? How will you treat your lover? Imagine how much ecstasy and passion you create in your communication and lovemaking. Do you hear music, see your self laughing and feeling close?

Adding the music that creates emotions of connection, passion, romance and love while you are visualizing all of the above really adds to the experience. Every time you hear this music, you will be associating and creating the vibrations of a relationship of your unique design into your mind. It's a simple technique that you can use to get yourself used to the feeling of being loved that is called an anchor. Each time you hear that music it will put you in an energy vibe of receptivity to love.

When you use this technique while you are in a heightened state, touch a spot on your body that you can easily have access to (squeeze your wrist, touch your heart, tap the back of your hand gently 3 times, or snap your fingers). You will be creating an anchor for that feeling in the future by touching that spot over and over until each time you touch there, you feel the emotions and sensations of this love in your heart and in your life!

By doing this exercise regularly you are creating a new internal message. This new internal message becomes a vibration that will send out a new signal corresponding with vibrations sent out by women with the same vibe, and you will connect somehow miraculously. It is mystical, real, and it works. You receive back your thoughts and vibrations! Try it! What do you have to gain? *LOVE! PASSION! MAGIC!* It's better than what you're doing now…right?

Only you know what your heart desires, and you can achieve that desire if you truly believe you deserve it and get your thoughts and energy aligned. Like a magnet, this alignment creates an invisible signal that attracts to us what we truly want — if the transmission isn't polluted with our own negativity we'll get results quickly.

Below is a list of descriptive adjectives to describe your ideal woman or yourself. These are also useful in creating a winning profile for online or off-line dating services, personal ads in the newspaper and telechat services! You can also use these adjectives to enhance your ad when you go online (millions of singles are connecting this way) and creatively describe what type of women you're looking for. The written word assists the subconscious mind in creating and manifesting your desires. You must conceive and believe it before you see it!

DESCRIPTIVE ADJECTIVES

accomplished	active	adorable
adventurous	agreeable	ambitious
amiable	ample	amusing
animated	appealing	ardent
aristocratic	articulate	artistic
assertive	assured	astute

athletic
balanced
bewitching
brawny
broad-minded
candid
oriented
chatty
compassionate
complex
conservative
cosmopolitan
creative
dainty
debonair
delightful
devilish
direct
down-to-earth
easygoing
elegant
energetic
enterprising
exquisite
exuberant
fearless
flamboyant
frisky
gallant
gifted
gracious
happy
honesty
husky
impish

attentive
bashful
boisterous
brazen
burly
captivating
cerebral
cheerful
communicative
congenial
considerate
courteous
cultured
daring
delicate
demure
dignified
discerning
earnest
eccentric
empathetic
enchanting
even-tempered
extraordinary
faithful
fiery
flexible
fun-loving
gentle
glamorous
graceful
hip
humanitarian
idealistic
impulsive

audacious
bawdy
bold
bright
buxom
career-
charming
chivalrous
classy
conscientious
convivial
crazy
curvaceous
dashing
deliberate
dependable
diligent
distinguished
earthy
educated
enchanting
energetic
ethical
extroverted
fascinating
finicky
frank
funny
genuine
good-natured
gregarious
homebody
humorous
idiosyncratic
independent

individualistic
introspective
jovial
liberal
lively
maverick
mischievous
natural
nonconformist
open-minded
original
outspoken
peppy
petite
poised
practical
rambunctious
reflective
reserved
reticent
roguish
saucy
self-assured
sensual
shapely
sociable
spirited
spry
steady
strong
sultry
tactful
tenacious
timid
tranquil

intelligent
intuitive
kooky
lighthearted
loyal
mellow
modest
naturalist
observant
opinionated
outrageous
particular
perceptive
playful
polished
pretty
rebellious
relaxed
responsible
risque
rowdy
seasoned
sensible
serene
sharp
sophisticated
spiritual
stable
stout
stylish
sunny
talented
tender
tolerant
trustworthy

intense
inventive
laid-back
literate
mature
merry
multifaceted
new age
old-fashioned
optimistic
outgoing
patient
personable
plump
positive
prosperous
refined
reliable
responsive
robust
rugged
secure
sensitive
serious
skillful
spicy
spontaneous
stately
strapping
substantial
supportive
talkative
thoughtful
traditional
unconven-

tional
vibrant
vigorous
vivacious
voluptuous
vulnerable
well-rounded
whimsical
willowy
witty
wise
worldly
young-at-heart
zany
zealous

Now we will work on the outside detailing of your vehicle to create a winning image....

PART TWO
THE EXTERNAL TUNE-UP

EXTERIOR CHECKLIST 6

"I usually make up my mind about a man in ten seconds, and I very rarely change it."

--Margaret Thatcher

HAVE YOU CHECKED YOUR CHASSIS LATELY?

CHECK OUT YOUR BODY

We have worked on your internal tuning and now it's time to take a look at your exterior. Knowing your best assets and accenting them is important. Your body is the vehicle that you ride in everyday. Are you taking care of it? Do you feel good about your body? We are now going to do a checkup on your physical appearance and the clothing you wear to enhance your body type and energy. Feeling good about your body is a must, and you don't have to have a perfect body to look your best. Having a good attitude and making the best of what gifts you have been given are key elements in your external tune-up.

Many men desire to be with a woman who is in great shape

and who looks put together in her clothes. Some men will check out and go after women who are more fit than they are, and wonder why those women aren't attracted to them physically. Have you given your body a good checkup lately? Are you what you are asking for? Do you have a big belly or love handles? Need to get in shape?

How do you expect us to check out your equipment if we can't see you under those extra pounds? Some women love "Teddy Bear" types, but don't expect most body-beautiful women to be falling all over you, if you're not in decent shape. Many women will overlook a few extra pounds, if you carry yourself well and dress tastefully. Wear clothing that flatters your body type.

Not all women are in perfect shape and being toned no matter what shape you have is important in the attraction phase of love and dating. If you are a big man and plan to stay that way, no problem just accent your strengths and best assets. I have a friend who has muscular wheels (great legs) and does his best to show them taste-fully. Do you know what your best features are? Your broad shoulders? Your rear end? (women do notice!) Your chest and arms? Your lean waistline? Show off your best features by wearing clothing that accentuates them! If you're a heavier man, wear clothing that fits and darker colors that slenderize.

You want to look your best because it reflects in your energy level when you're out. If you're not proficient in choosing the proper clothing, there are many books you can read on dressing properly, or choose a professional to take you shopping. In my business, I take many clients shopping and may add only a few items to spruce up their wardrobes. All of my clients have reported feeling more together and they definitely got more positive responses from women by having their look together. Try it!

Eating habits and regular workouts add to your overall sex-appeal and your magnetic powers of attracting women. If you desire guidance with your diet, contact your local nutrition specialist or fitness center and find a person to work with who will support you with your unique fitness program. Get to the gym, go for a walk everyday; just a 30-minute workout will improve your attitude and add some tone to your body. Use the Energy Tools (in Chapter 10) to maximize your performance.

It depends on what kind of work you do, and yet what you wear does have an impact. How do you present yourself to the world everyday? How do you carry yourself? The way you walk is important, and your posture is a clear sign of your confidence level. Stand tall, shoulders back, sit up in your chair, and you'll project more confidence and feel better about your initial approach.

Am I starting to sound like your mother? Sorry! I'm here to help!

Believe it or not, according to all the surveys, a man's shoes are a big part of his first impression. What kind of shoes do you wear most of the time? Get rid of shoes that are beat up and worn, because you will look unpolished and sloppy (unless that is your look or goal).

Your choice in clothing and the way that you wear it shows others your style, and labels you a certain type.

- *The casual style*
- *The conservative yuppie*
- *The business suit*
- *The classic style*
- *The sporty jock*
- *The earthy hippie*
- *The grungy mess*
- *The sexy Casanova*
- *The frump*
- *The trendy streetwear type*
- *Styleless*

Once you discover your sense of style, this will help you to define the kind of woman that you want to connect with. Are you a more casual-type guy, or are you a business man? You need to figure out the kind of woman you want to attract, and wear clothing that enhances your assets and creates a winning image.

How you present yourself is how you are perceived by the

world — especially women. So, if you're a casual-type guy, and you want to meet a classy, beautiful woman, it's OK if you're casual, but most attractive women take noticeably good care of themselves and enjoy spending time with a put-together man! They take care of their hands, their skin, their hair, and men say, *"Wow! She's beautiful! How can I attract her?"* These women want a man who takes care of himself. Taking care of your outside detailing is vital to attracting most women.

Women do look at everything about you: your hands, your accessories, your skin and your hair. You may notice her jewelry and accessories and think, She's really put together, and think to yourself, *"Uh oh, I'm in trouble. She looks like she's too much for me."* You judge a woman when you first see her, right? Do you have an instant judgment of what she's like? You bet! We do the same thing. We think, *"He obviously doesn't work out. He doesn't take care of himself. He's pretty good-looking, but he's awfully scruffy."* Or *"Wow he is put together! A man with style! I wonder if he is available?"*

CLOTHES THAT WILL CREATE
THE BEST IMPRESSION

Your sense of style has a lot to do with how confident you feel about yourself. I realize most men do not like to be told what to wear. I'm just passing on the message I have heard from hundreds of women. If you are already stylin' in your current attire, then skip this section! I suggest finding out your colors from a specialist in that field (color analysis), because some colors make you feel sexier and look more alive. You can get swatches to take shopping with you, so you know you are choosing the right things for your skin tones and hair color. The cost for color analysis is $100-$200, or you could buy a book on the subject — *Color for Men* and *Color Me Beautiful* — both by Carol Jackson. To look healthier and more powerful, discover shades of color in clothes to compliment your natural skin tones and hair color. Color can also change your energy state.

For those of you who don't have an extensive wardrobe and want to spruce yours up, here are some suggestions. These are the wardrobe basics to mix and match for the proper occasion. By having these pieces you will always be ready for any occasion from a formal affair, to a brief coffee date, to a romantic picnic in the park. This section does not include grunge wear.

WARDROBE BASICS

* A basic pair of black, navy, and or khaki pants (many materials out now are wrinkle free)
* A few crisp white shirts (with or without a collar, depending on current styles)
* A few casual shirts -- silk, cotton, or flannel (for colder climates)
* The over shirt to wear with T-shirts underneath (Gap, Banana Republic, Urban Outfitters)
* Jeans that fit you well (blue jean and black are perfect basics)
* A nice leather jacket
* A man must have a basic black, gray or dark suit for special occasions and for more formal events
* An overcoat that is basic to wear in cold weather
* A few basic T-shirts in colors that complement your skin tone to wear under sweaters or blazers (Banana Republic™, The Gap™, and most better department stores have a varied selection nationwide.)
* Sweaters in V or crew necklines are always in style when you buy basic designs. Buy sweaters that are soft to the touch (cashmere is great!)
* Casual blazers (bright colors, if you're brave) to wear with jeans or slacks
* A basic, unstructured, black, navy or neutral blazer can really dress up jeans/casual slacks
* Crew or turtleneck sweaters/basic cotton sweaters
* A few pairs of exercise/casual shorts and tee shirts that coordinate
* Lounge wear: sweats, zip-up sweat jacket, sweat shirts (women love to wear them), pajamas in soft cotton

- *Nice underwear (no stains or rips) – boxers, briefs, sport briefs (Silk or soft cotton will make you more touchable.)*
- *A pair of basic black and/or brown dress shoes (In a survey, hundreds of women claimed that the first thing they looked at when "checking out" a man were his shoes.)*
- *A pair of black and/or brown casual shoes to wear with jeans or casual wear*
- *Socks — that are color-coordinated with your clothing/shoes (designs are attractive depending on the event)*
- *Athletic shoes — sneakers, tennis shoes, cross-trainers (If you are wearing them to go somewhere other than the gym, make sure they're clean! I do not recommend wearing sneakers on a date, unless, of course, it is an athletic date, such as playing tennis, hiking etc.... Of course, it depends on the type of woman, and it depends on the kind of date you're going on.)*
- *Boots — the current trend or cowboy boots (never go out of style depending on where you live)*
- *Hiking Boots and work boots for casual clothing (a cool look)*
- *Sandals for warmer weather — There are the dressy, woven, European leather sandals, and then the Birkenstock™/Teva™ types for comfort. Make sure they are not beat up or ripped.*
- *A soft cotton robe to wear after a shower or bath.*

If you have some of these basics, are they worn out? Out dated? Washed out from laundering? Just buying a few items such as fresh white T-shirts, a new pair of black slacks, or a blazer will freshen your wardrobe.

DETAILING
ACCESSORIES MAKE THE MAN

Let's face it guys, you don't have as many accessories to spruce up your wardrobe as women do, so pick them carefully. These items pull an outfit together and show your unique style. Your age group and sense of style will make each man chose differently. These are the basic accessories to consider adding to your wardrobe to pull it all together. By having good accessories, you can make less expensive clothing look more appealing and have more options when getting dressed to impress.

♦ *Belts and shoes in matching color and leather quality.*
♦ *Watches are accessories that definitely make a statement about your style.*
♦ *Eyewear. Glasses and sunglasses are among the most visible accessories and show your individual taste. Some men wear sunglasses and watches as symbols of status. If you desire to appear more successful, these accessories will add the "style" element to your wardrobe*
♦ *For the businessman, a sharp briefcase is imperative*
♦ *For the trendy man, a clean leather or cloth tote bag or backpack is styling.*
♦ *Ties that show your uniqueness (great conversation starters)*
♦ *Suspenders always add some flair*
♦ *Vests are evidence of your individuality and are great conversation "icebreakers."*
♦ *Tasteful jewelry: A classic simple ring, college ring and family rings are classic. What ever is tasteful for your style, and that may change over the years as you discover what that style is for you. Earrings, beads, tattoos and body piercing are fine (if that is the image you'd like to project) and yet many trends go in and out of style quickly. Many men don't wear much jewelry and if you do, coordinate the metal color with your watch metal color. If you wear more jewelry, don't overdo it, unless you're a rock star or want a lot of attention.*
♦ *Cell phones with unique tones and covers are also conversation starters.*
♦ *Hats are also a great addition to any outfit, if combined properly. Wearing a unique hat stands out and catches the eye.*

Every man should have a full-length mirror somewhere in his home to check himself out and make sure all his clothes are lined up, matching, and the zippers are zipped. (The mirror over the bed does not count.) Women will appreciate it when they are dressing or undressing at your place. This may not be important to you, but women will notice!

Guys have a tendency to wear their favorite thing over and over, like their favorite shirt, shoes or belt. When you are meeting a woman that you're really attracted to, you want to make sure that your accessories match and that you don't repeat outfits date after date. I dated a man who wore the same pants four dates in a row. I thought it strange that he didn't notice. This is a detail that some men overlook. If you don't have money to buy extra clothing, just make sure they are clean. You can also shop at resale designer stores if you are on a budget.

WASHING AND WAXING BASICS

When you take a bath or a shower, you could use the newest body scrubs with moisturizers, and lightly apply oil to your body to assist with dry skin. It is highly suggested to use body lotion/oil on your body, because we're the ones feeling your body (hopefully), and we would like it to be soft. When you touch a woman, she feels soft and usually smells good. The reason women use body moisturizers, creams and perfumes is to feel good and to take care of themselves. Some women prepare "as if" they have a man desiring to rub their soft skin. Have your skin ready to be touched!

The body washes on the market today don't have a lot of scents, so you will still smell like a man. In the winter, or in dry heat, your skin can get really dry, especially your arms and legs, and obviously, your face, so you want to make sure your skin is well lubed. You can go to your local drugstore or health food store and buy body lotion, preferably without mineral oil (Aveeno is an excellent choice). Believe me, if you have lotions, oils, body scrubs around when a woman comes to your home, she will think, *Hey, he really takes care of himself,* and you might even get her to spend the night, because she'll feel at home with some of the products she needs and uses daily.

Also, when showering, it is important to use a washcloth and soap to thoroughly cleanse those intimate parts, particularly your backside. Freshen up those private parts and clean up before the night begins. Believe me, women are highly aware of your body odors, especially during intimacy. Using deodorant is a must.

SKIN CARE BASICS

Women want a man who takes good care of his skin. Facials are a natural and wonderful overhaul to brighten and even your skin tones. Women will admire that you take good care of the largest organ on your body, and you'll love the pampering. It's very relaxing and stimulating to the skin. The well-kept man cleanses his skin everyday and uses a Sun Protection Factor (SPF) 15 moisturizer. Using Shaving gels and a good moisturizer will keep you looking more vibrant. Just as the exterior of your car needs wax to protect the paint from the elements, so does your skin.

Women talk amongst themselves: *"Tell me, what does he look like? His skin is dried out, and his hair looks like a mess, but you could work on him."* So, it's important to take care of your skin. Consider incorporating a basic skin-care system into your daily grooming regime, like my new Skin Care System for Men. This line was uniquely designed to enhance the overall appearance of your skin. Check it out on my site if you really want to improve your appearance and get that edge to compete in the dating game. Women will long to touch your skin!

A regular manicure is a plus, especially for a man who works with his hands. Many women look at your hands. When a man shakes a woman's hand, the first thing they think is, *Are his hands soft? Would I want him touching my body with those dry hands?* Do you have clean nails? What about your feet? Don't overlook your feet just because they are out of sight. There are instances that women will come in contact with your bare feet, check out your feet and toe nails. Do they smell? Getting manicures and pedicures is not an unusual thing to do in these times. If you're really smart, you'll go often, because there are always women there, and they love it when a man walks in. *"Oh my God, a man that takes care of himself!"* You may end up being fixed up with all of the single women there, because manicurists are notorious matchmakers (hairdressers, too). They usually say, *"Are you married?"* If you reply, *"No, I'm not,"* they'll say to their female clients, *"You should see this guy who comes in on Saturday mornings. He's really cute."* They love to report your single status to all their favorite, available female clients and many love connections have occurred in nail salons.

SELF-SERVICE AND QUICK FIXES
FOR YOUR HAIR

If you want your hair to feel and smell good, professional products sold in salons and beauty supply stores do make a difference. The Paul Mitchell™ line is a great line with all the products you will need for hair styling.

There are always women in beauty supply stores, and it's a great place to meet them. You could ask, *"Excuse me, can you suggest something I could use on my hair?"* The condition of your hair (whether it's dry, oily, or normal) will determine the type of products you should use. For men who want to wear their hair slicked back or want more control (if your hair is a little flyaway), you can put a little sculpting lotion in your hair to keep it looking good. Now there are many pomades and texturizing gels available that will keep dry or curly hair in place. Go get samples if you're not sure which one to buy.

A professional haircut is one of your most important exterior accessories, so choose your hairstylist carefully. Don't be cheap when it comes to your haircut because a bad haircut can take months to grow out. Look at other men who have the same type of hair, and, if you like their cut, ask them who cuts their hair. If you get a bushy neckline in between haircuts, you can stop by a salon or barbershop and have them trim it, or you can trim it yourself at home with your razor.

Many men are self-conscious about thinning hair and are considering hair restoration. Now, with new technology, the results are amazing! There are so many options you can explore. The consultations are free. What do you have to lose?

Facial hair? Apply conditioner on your beard when you shower and keep your beard trimmed with home trimmers. Kissing with a rough face is hard on a woman's skin, so beware of the shorter beards unless your woman can take it. . .be gentle. It's a must to be aware of nasal hairs and any hairs around your ears. There are nose-hair trimmers that make it simple to keep your nose and ears clean. If you are very hairy, laser technology is extraordinarily successful in permanent hair removal (even ear hair). If you have bushy eyebrows, you can have them easily shaped at a salon without embarrassment — ask your hairstylist. Hair removal products such as Nad's™ is the best on the market for removing unwanted hair.

Keeping your lips in shape is also important, and lip balm is just what you need to keep those lips in tip-top working order. There is something about soft, kissable lips that will keep us coming back for more. By the way, kissing is the key to building intimacy and igniting the passion in women. We can tell how passionate a man is by his kissing skills.

The first kiss is the key to opening the door to a woman's heart.

EXHAUST FUMES

There is nothing worse than a man with bad breath and stained teeth. When you're out meeting women and you know that you have coffee, alcohol, and/or cigarette breath, always carry mints in your pocket. We've all encountered people with "death breath". Whenever you see them coming, you just have to run away because if they come too close, you'd die!

Everyone should evaluate their teeth and breath. With all of the products available now and proper hygiene: brushing, flossing, regular checkups, teeth whiteners and straighteners, and the laser technology — it is easy to improve the appearance of your teeth. Here is some info from Dr. Richard Spragg, a popular holistic dentist in Beverly Hills, California:

"As a dentist, unfortunately, our noses and senses get trained a little bit more to halitosis or bad breath, and I'd say that would

be one of the first issues you would deal with when it comes to close encounters. In fact, I was out at Chin Chin's last week, and an older gentleman was sitting there on a first date, and he had the worst breath. I could smell him from a table away, and I just couldn't imagine him ever progressing further with his date. Through good old hygiene, getting your teeth cleaned every four to six months and using products such as Breath Rx (which is a combination of a mouth rinse, toothpaste, tongue scrapers) allows you to fight what's causing the problem. He had a problem, and it won't go away by itself. Most of the smells we get are emitted more from the gums than the tongue, so if you eliminate the bacterial infection in the gums through proper cleaning, then scrape your tongue and use the proper rinses, you're able to eliminate the malodor.

"When it comes to the aesthetics of a smile (whether they're straight, crooked, and so forth), whenever someone comes in my office, the first thing I give them is a self-smile evaluation. I give them a sheet, and I say, "Evaluate your own smile," and I say, "What do you like about it? What do you dislike about it? Are there any things you want to change? We then use imaging machines in which we cosmetically image their teeth right there in the office. Then we'll take a picture of their teeth, and put it up on our TV monitor, and their teeth are 20 x 20, and when you see your teeth that large, sometimes you don't realize, "Oh my gosh, my teeth are really yellow!" or "My teeth are really crooked," and you'll see imperfections that dentists can see.

"Just showing them how you can improve their smiles, or maybe help increase their self-esteem, because you find a lot of people who aren't smilers — they'll lip smile, or they'll put their hand over their mouth, because they have a lower self-esteem about their smile — but once that's corrected, you'll see a metamorphosis in people. They change their hairstyle, they get contact lenses, and they can become a completely new person. That's the beautiful thing about cosmetic dentistry, and unlike orthodontics or braces, rather than taking months and years, you could have it

done in weeks, so they could have incredible results and you could actually change people's lives completely. I say your smile and your breath are going to be the two major factors that are going make you or break you on a date."

You don't have to have perfect teeth, but regular flossing and cleaning by your hygienist (who will also fix you up with her best friend) will enhance your breath, as well, and give you a clean, bright smile. Just do it!

JUST THE SCENT OF YOU

Most women are turned on by scents, and it is vital to be aware of your body odor. Colognes do not cover up bad body odor. Day colognes are usually citrus-based, athletic-type scents, i.e., CK One™, Cool Water™, Infinity™, Nautica™, and evening colognes are usually heavier, like Drakkar Noir™ , Armani™, Obsession™, and Fahrenheit™. There are always new and exciting scents coming out on the market, including essential oils, that can be bought at your local heath food store. Apply according to the strength of the cologne or oil and how it smells on you. Take a poll...ask women if they enjoy your cologne.

The scent of a clean man, even without cologne, is intoxicating to some women — your pheromones alone can drive women wild! The smell of a man can be the chemistry factor that makes a woman stick around a little longer to get to know you better.

MORE EXHAUST FUMES

The types of exhaust fumes we would like you to be aware of are belching and/or "breaking wind." If exhaust fumes are inevitable, walk away quickly for the former or leave the room for the latter. If it has to happen during an intimate moment, please give us fair warning.

Now that we have you detailed — looking sharp, feeling confident and smelling magnificent – let's check out your living space....

PARKING YOUR VEHICLE 7

"Build it and they will come!"

--Field of Dreams

IS YOUR HOME READY FOR LOVE?

If the lover of your dreams showed up today, how would you feel about the appearance of your living space? If you knew that your mate was coming into your life soon, would you make some adjustments to your home or apartment?

The place where you live can make you feel depressed when it's not together. Where you live is where you relax, rejuvenate, and think thoughts that are "energy lifting" or "energy draining." It helps to live in an environment that makes you feel good when you come home to regenerate. Does your home reflect how you feel about yourself? Don't wait until you meet someone to get it ready. Prepare it now, and she will come. Once again...*Act As If...*

After meeting you, dates come to check you out at the place where you live. Take a look at what your home looks like right now. Is it an environment that a date would enjoy spending time? Is it an environment that you feel proud to call home? Can you comfortably say to your date, *"I'd like to invite you back to my place and show you where I live?"*

WHAT IS YOUR HOME OR APARTMENT LIKE RIGHT NOW?

Are you prepared? Your home reflects how you feel about yourself. Do you feel comfortable there? Take a look around. Is it a mess? Neat, but boring? Empty? Cluttered? Dirty? Does it need painting or some new tiles in the kitchen? What could you improve on? Do you need help being more creative? Do you have a little extra money on hand to fix it up?

Write a list of the things you could do right now to improve your living environment ask yourself:

♦ *As you walk in the front door, is your home presentable?*
♦ *How does it smell?*
♦ *Which rooms do you spend the most time in alone?*
♦ *If you were to be involved with someone, would you have a room they could relax in and hang out with you?*
♦ *Do you have music to set a mood? Soft lighting?*
♦ *Is your place even set up to have someone visit? Is there ambiance? Is there romance? I'm not saying it has to be filled with flowers and romantic pictures, but is it clean?*
♦ *Which room do you want to work on first?*

Most people detest bright lights. You don't need to spend a lot of money on lighting, but surely invest in dimmer switches that you can install yourself. When an interested woman walks into your living space, the first thing she will usually do is walk around and say to herself, *"Hmm, he keeps a nice place. He takes care of himself. I'm impressed."* Or she thinks, *"I could put my stuff in here. My rug would look good there."* Or, *"Help, I'm outta here. This person is a mess!"* A first impression is a lasting one.

Is your home in a safe neighborhood? Is it convenient to get

to? Close to fun things for a single person to do? If not, get someone to help you find a neighborhood that will support your single
life. Get a female friend to help you add some flare to your bach-
elor lair or hire a designer. Check out my recommended referrals
online if you need assistance with home decor, repairs or painting.

DATES DO CHECK OUT YOUR BATHROOM.

Women will and do like to look around. Then, they eventually
visit your bathroom. Is there scum and mold in your shower? Are
hairs stuck to the sides of your sink? Is your bathroom clean? Do
you have any toilet paper? If they happen to look in your cabinet
and see that you have body lotion and other supplies you use to take
care of yourself, they'll think, *"Yes! He takes care of himself, and
this place is clean...this man is together and confident."*

Just having a new bath mat, a fresh shower curtain and a
few new towels that coordinate can spruce up your bathroom.
Hiring a maid is also the answer for men that detest cleaning. A
once a month visit is a life saver!

COMFORTABLE INTERIORS

Women love to see that you take care of yourself, because then
they can believe they'll be safe and comfortable in your company.
It's not about expensive, flashy furniture or things, but how your
home is tastefully "put together." A comfortable seating area for
snuggling is essential. Select a couch that is comfortable, soft against
your skin, and large enough for at least two. There is nothing worse
than an itchy or cold couch, especially if you're getting romantic
and have bare skin exposed. Even worse is an uncomfortable, slouch-
ing couch that will put you close together but sinks when you sit in
it. For those with a horrid covering but a great sturdy couch, go to
a bed and bath store for a cover to fit your couch, and you can
transform a room for around $100-$400. This will depend on your
budget, where you shop, and checking out sales and discount stores.

Create your home as you would if you were in love, and when

you're at home alone, listen to romantic music, light some candles, create the ambiance, and get into the energy state of being with a lover. *Act As If.* People come visit me at my place, and I have candles lit most of the time, and the house smells great. They will comment, *"Do you have a hot date or something?"* I always say *"Why does it mean that if my home setting is romantic, I have a hot date? This is just how I live!"* If you do this, a lover will eventually show up, and they will be thrilled, because being in that environment comes naturally to you! You will be prepared to warm up their engines!

BEDROOM TUNE-UP

If you have personal things that belong to an ex — jewelry, garters, lingerie — or pictures of her, put them away where your new friend cannot see them. Do you have too many clothes and junk strewn all over the place? What about your sheets? Would you bring a lover into your bed? Some men have scruffy, itchy bedding, and it's a turnoff. Some women tell me how nice it is to sleep in soft, clean sheets at a man's house, other women express shock at how men past 30 years old still have sheets from college. This ensemble includes the old flannel blankets and lumpy pillows.

One successful man I dated had a very uncomfortable bed, and I decided I would never sleep over after my experience there. We were watching a football game at his place, and I wanted to nap, so I asked to go into his room so I could fall asleep and be more re-laxed. It was the worst! The room was cold; the sheets were itchy and smelled bad. I had to ask him, *"Do you sleep in this bed? How can you get any rest here?"* He said he was waiting until he met someone to help him pick out new things. We went shopping the next day, and I helped him set up his new bedroom ensemble. He was so happy and felt so proud that he made me happy. He always thanks me for assisting him and says his bed is a lot more comfort-able and I'm sure the woman currently in his life will think so too!

Make sure that where you sleep is comfortable for you and for your lover. If she is spending the night, try to keep the room on the warm side, especially if you like a window open for fresh air. Some women don't like being cold when they are sleeping over. Many men say they hate too many heavy blankets because they sometimes feel confined — it's a good idea to have an extra in case we get cold.

When you visit a woman, you'll notice candles, perfume and feminine touches. It is pleasant when a man notices these things and compliments her good taste.

As you prepare for love to come, you want your home environment to be welcoming to a new romance and you want it comfortable for yourself. You want your home to be a good place to rest, write, create, do your hobbies, watch sports or movies, listen to music, read, do your visualization work and relax.

When you're setting the tone for love, you want to feel and look your best and have an environment that makes a woman feel comfortable.

Color is the secret to a good image for yourself and can make a difference in your home environment. Discover the colors that make you look your best before you start redecorating your place or buying new clothing as mentioned in the last chapter. Spend the money to learn what colors are best for your skin tones and that make you feel good. Wall colors, drapery, sheets, bedding, and bathroom colors are important to create a warm living environment.

When you arrive at your new love nest, you can turn some great music on to set the mood. You might have a few candles around and some incense or aromatherapy dispensers. If you need ideas on romantic music, go to your local music store — there is a whole romance section in many stores now— or check the Internet.

Un-Clutter Your Space.

If your home is a mess, no problem – you can either hire somebody for a couple of hours to clean up for you, or do it yourself. Make time in your schedule to organize your closets, and you'll get all psyched up to free up space in your life. Clutter in your home reflects in your energy. It slows down your creativity when things are stacked up around you. You can't focus clearly and your mind starts to create "to do" lists. You may feel overwhelmed. Start slowly. Clean up the first place in your house that is causing you to stress out and lose energy. Is it your desk? Your bedroom? The whole place? *CALL FOR HELP*!

It's a really great feeling to get rid of old clutter, papers and things you don't use anymore! Bills and papers can be easily separated in stackable files, and you can have a clear desk to work on. Or get a file cabinet and create files for those loose pieces of paper with numbers on them. Do one clean-up at a time. Holding on to some sentimental things is okay, but if you are living in a small space, have a small storage space available to keep them so they aren't always staring you in the face, because it drains your energy. If you absolutely cannot detach from things, organize them and keep them in one area of your home (a closet, storage space, or garage).

THE NUTS AND BOLTS YOU'LL NEED TO ORGANIZE YOURSELF:

For your office or work space just go pick up a few items to get organized. Having the right equipment makes the job flow easier.

- *File cabinet(s)*
- *Files with labels*
- *Boxes for storage*
- *Large envelopes to store papers that you want to keep (tax papers, business transactions, letters, memoirs and bills for filing)*
- *Photo albums for those pictures still left in the original package*
- *A marker to label everything*
- *Stackable paper separators, tape, paper clips and a stapler to organize papers that need your attention*

One day, work on your desk, or do it in increments of time. Piece by piece you'll get it completed and feel relieved. By having all the supplies, you'll be ready to move the extra papers into a box for storage or in files. No excuses!

Before you organize your clothing and accessories you will need the following items:

- *Large heavy plastic bags with ties (for all the old clothing you'll be donating to charity or giving away)*
- *A few empty boxes for glass and heavier items*
- *Shoe trees for your new shoes*
- *Tie and belt racks*
- *Suit hangers*

Clean out your old clothes, shoes, and all the junk that is taking up space, and make some space for "her." Donate them, give them to a friend who needs them and rid yourself of clothing that has bad memories and brings you down. Remember those "too-tight-to-feel-great-in" items. If you haven't fit in your jeans in a few years get rid of them and buy a pair that fits. You will never miss them once they are out of sight. Those clothes that are a color that you question, put them aside and have a friend whose taste you trust come by to give you a second opinion. If you are new to the area, call a wardrobe/color consultant to help you with this – for the fee, it will be worth every penny when you're wearing only things that make you look and feel great! Get rid of old shoes and sneakers that don't reflect your image or are rough around the edges.

Do you ever feel great in a color and have only a few items in your closet that people constantly comment about? They make you feel more confident and sexy, so wear them! Don't wait to meet a hot woman to wear the right clothes. Wear them now! Act as if you're going to meet a woman every time you go out and take a look at yourself on the way out the door. Every day and anywhere is an opportunity to meet people so look your best, even when you're going out for a quick trip to the store. You never know where you might run into a woman that might interest you. Your style leaves a lasting impression. Make it a great one!

INTERIOR CHECKLIST
FOR YOUR LIVING SPACE

These are the items women will notice when arriving at your home and these also create lasting impressions.

PICTURES: Pictures of your family and friends around your home show you are sentimental.

BOOKS: Your interests and hobbies revealed.

MUSIC: CDs, tapes, and records express your taste in music and your style.

TASTEFUL ART: Sculptures, paintings and well-crafted, artistic furniture show both your financial status and your taste. Your art could be contemporary, classic or periodic. Art is such an individual expression and sometimes less is more.

SPORTS EQUIPMENT/ACCESSORIES: Self-explanatory and great conversation pieces.

FURNITURE: Your furniture reflects your style and it is so important to have a place to entertain women and friends when they stop by. A couch or seating area is normally the first thing that people see when arriving at your place.

POTS AND PANS: A decent set of pots and pans are always a plus. Especially if you plan to cook for your dates or you enjoy cooking in general. Even just a basic set is great for the easy to cook items…omelets, broiling chicken or fish and making pasta!

COFFEE MAKER OR TEA POT: To make hot beverages for your guests when you are relaxing at home.

DISHES AND SILVERWARE: A basic set of decent dishes and silverware is a must. A matching set of 4 is a good start and is relatively inexpensive. Rid yourself of dishes and cups that are cracked or chipped.

GLASSES, COFFEE MUGS AND WINE GLASSES: For the refreshments you will serve when guests arrive.

BASIC KITCHEN UTENSILS: Bottle openers, can opener, spatula, serving bowls for salads and vegetables and serving spoons.

TROPHIES, AWARDS AND DIPLOMAS: A smart conversation

starter and non-intrusive way to get to learn about someone's life.

MOVIES: Videotapes and Laser Discs tell a lot about your personality and what era you're from and the types of movies you enjoy.

COMPUTER GAMES: Nintendo/Sega Genesis or hand-held electronic games. How techno are you?

PLANTS: Are they alive? Or wilting?

ANIMALS: Do you have pets? Are they clean? Dates watch how you treat your animals as a good reflection of patience and child-rearing skills, because to some people their animals are their kids. Do you clean up after them? If you don't like your date's pet(s), that could present a problem for a long-term relationship, and animal allergies are no fun to deal with. There are new shots and some homeopathic remedies available to counterbalance animal allergies.

Next is the list of items that woman appreciate you having around especially if you want us to stay overnight. Sometimes having some of these items can be a deal closer when you want her to stay over.

CHECKLIST OF THINGS WOMEN APPRECIATE:
- *Romantic music*
- *Nice soft towels*
- *Clean face cloths*
- *A blow dryer*
- *A clean shower curtain and bath tub*
- *Contact lens solution and a container for her lenses*
- *Q-tips*
- *Tissues*
- *Cotton balls*
- *Body lotion/oil*
- *Bubble Bath/oils/Massage oils*
- *Extra toothbrush/toothpaste*
- *Aspirin/Tylenol/Advil*

- *Brush/Comb*
- *Moisturizer for her face (Skin Mechanix would be perfect!)*
- *Good shampoo and conditioner*
- *Sharp razor/Shaving Cream/Gel*
- *Mirrors, especially full-length mirrors*
- *Clean terry-cloth bathrobe or something for her to sleep in*
- *Air freshener spray in the bathroom*
- *Candles and matches/lighter*
- *Soft lighting*
- *Soft warm blanket for when she is cold*
- *Nice glasses for romantic moments*
- *Chocolate or something sweet*
- *Chilled fresh juices, sparkling water, champagne, beers, coffee/tea, any of her favorite drinks/snacks*
- *Fresh flowers! Anytime, anywhere, WE LOVE FLOWERS!*
- *Men with tools (there is something to be said about a man that has a tool box)*

It's great to ask women what they enjoy eating, drinking and their favorite desserts and to keep some "in stock." Remembering her favorite sweets or foods is impressive. How does she take her tea or coffee? Do you know if she drinks coffee or sodas? When you're dating someone with special food allergies or diet restrictions, remember the items that she can or cannot have when cooking or taking her out to dine. This act shows her you were listening and are sensitive to her special needs, and that goes a long way in the consideration department.

Feeling good about your home is a confidence builder. How do you feel about yours? Your home is a great place to start to prepare for love.

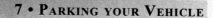

Now let's explore your chosen career path and how this affects your life and relationships....

DAILY COMMUTE

"Go confidently in the direction of your dreams.

Live the life you have imagined."

--Henry David Thoreau

IS YOUR WORK/CAREER WORTH LEAVING THE HOUSE FOR?

Some men spend almost one-half of their lives working. Do you love your career? What you do for a living and how you speak about it is really important. Many women have told me, "When I asked him what kind of work he did, he said, *"Well, I don't know. I'm not really sure. I'm just kind of bored and not really clear on where I'm headed right now."* The initial conversation you have with a woman makes a big difference in her mind — especially if she is impassioned with what she does and you're not. Remember those first conversations activate a lasting impression. You know how you feel when a woman doesn't have a sense of direction, right? Some women might think, *"He doesn't have his act together."* You've lost the game before it ever began.

PEOPLE CAN READ YOUR VERBAL MESSAGES ABOUT YOUR WORK.

It doesn't necessarily matter what you do, whether you're retired, looking for something new, in a job that is just providing financial support for you to pursue your dreams or you think your job is fantastic. What matters is your attitude about your work. If you're working to pay the bills and hate it, just reword how you communicate that in your initial conversations with people. As mentioned before, the first impression is a lasting one. According to Dale Carnegie, *"You never achieve real success, unless you like what you're doing."* People look for enthusiasm when you talk about your work. Unless you work at home, your work is also a great source for meeting other singles.

Go see a career coach, counselor or attend seminars that offer career testing if you need ideas and motivation in the work-related fields. If you find you are not satisfied with your work, it might be time to ask yourself some of these questions and do a work alignment.

WORK ALIGNMENT

ASK YOURSELF THESE QUESTIONS TO CHECK YOUR BELIEFS ABOUT YOUR WORK:

- *Am I being compensated fairly for my work?*
- *Do I like the place where I work?*
- *Do I enjoy the people I work with?*
- *Is my work fulfilling and challenging?*
- *Am I creating balance between my work and my playtime?*
- *Does my work serve a greater purpose for me?*
- *Have I taken the initiative to investigate more fulfilling possibilities?*
- *What work would I be doing if I could do whatever I wanted?*
- *What actions can I take to make my work more exciting?*
- *Are my conversations at work supporting my goals?*
- *Is it time to move on in my career and check out new jobs?*

If you're still searching for your life's work, no problem. I strongly suggest to do activities that do turn you on, even part-time. If you're curious about a life-style or job, investigate the most successful person (or organization) that interests you. Find some way to get in the door. Ask for a job or volunteer to work for free a few hours a week. Ask happy people with good energy what they enjoy about their careers. Find out what they've learned so far.

Don't sit there waiting for the ideas to land in your lap. Go and explore any and all of those things about which you say, *"Maybe someday, I'll..."* Do those things until you discover a new passion. When you are out expressing yourself, you will come into contact with opportunities you may have never thought of before. While out exploring, keep your conversations positive when you first meet someone — it will turn others off if you whine about being broke and unfocused.

I personally followed my own advice and each adventure led me to the next, and I met amazing people along the way. I asked a lot of questions of those people who loved what they did, and I got guidance from many who were willing to share their wisdom with me. My curiosity led me to my work and I learned about many different types of career possibilities that I might have missed.

I remember I always wanted to be on TV and do commercials, and so I took a course many years ago at Weist Barron™ in Philadelphia. I loved it! Subsequently, I studied marketing, physiology, human communications and the healing arts to keep my mind sharp. I learned TV editing and all aspects of production. I then interviewed many of the experts in the relationships industry on the radio and I kept exploring new avenues of interest until I found what turned me on the most. Today I'm an author, personal relationship coach, columnist and seminar leader. I never imagined this would be my path. My life changed the day I was asked to speak to men about loving women. In combination with the skills I had learned (and continue to learn), this created a new career path for me, and it has been a total creative adventure ever since. When people ask me how I came to do my coaching/consulting/speaking/ TV/radio work,

I just say *"I was led there by fate."* I love sharing the life changing experiences and the insights of the influential people I have interviewed that led me to my work. I now guide and assist people to achieve fast results without having to go through some of the road blocks I have experienced. This work is so rewarding for me because by sharing my truth, it helps others discover new possibilities for themselves. Here is a true story about a client who believed he had found his life's work and what he discovered along his path.

One of my long-standing clients was determined to become a lawyer. For years, he worked full-time while attending law school. Finally, he completed his mission! He was both excited and exhausted from the grueling schedule in school. To his dismay, once he got into it, he found that he hated the work. He realized that he did it only to be able to call himself an attorney and receive the prestige that comes with the title. He got frustrated and sick from the stress, and he didn't enjoy the firm he was working for, or the people that worked with him. The environment affected his health and personal life to a point of deep depression. He saw how horrid that life-style can be and the stress it caused his coworkers, and he couldn't find enough role models to emulate. His energy kept getting lower and lower because he wasn't fulfilled inside. We discussed his options and began using the same principals to finding love to discovering his new working environment.

He began looking into other fields, exploring other ways to utilize his education and earn a living in a more supportive environment. I suggested he explore other areas of interest so he got involved in the Natural Law Party, started taking dance lessons and volunteered for different causes. Instead of sulking he was taking action! There was a stronger balance in his life between fun and work, so his job didn't seem as bad while he searched for a new direction. While he was doing his exploring, he met many interesting people that led him in new directions utilizing all of his talents and interests. He had been writing out his goals and telling people his new vision instead of whining about hating his job. He looked and spoke more positively about his future and is now sure that the education he worked so hard for will pay off. He opened himself to new opportunities with a refreshed attitude and they showed up. He not only got a great job, he met his life partner along the way!

GOSSIP AND ENERGY LEAKS AT WORK

The things you say about yourself to people you work with is key to keeping your life on a more positive level and not causing unnecessary gossip. The people you work with are a part of your daily life, and if you go to work saying, *"I can't meet anybody, I don't know anybody, and I'm really lonely,"* then they'll probably think of you as a loser and will chat about your misfortune at work. The last thing you say to a person is most likely what they will remember. For instance, if you tell me, *"I can't stand my job, and I'm really lonely,"* the next time I see you, I'm going to think *There's the lonely guy who doesn't like his job.* That thought has been implanted in my mind about you.

Here's a real conversation with a woman friend. Nickie says, *"I just broke up with Aaron, and I'm miserable, and to top it all off, I'm broke."* Guess what? Even though she may get back together with Aaron and get a new job, for the next month, you are talking/thinking about *"Poor Nickie. She broke up with Aaron, and she's broke."* Everyone you talk to that day (who knows her and cares) about her relationship and her financial situation is also thinking these "low energy and negative" thoughts about her. What a shame, because those comments may only have been true for a couple of hours!

Be very careful about what you say to people about yourself. If you say, *"I'm creating a new business now, I'm excited and my Life is Good!"*, then that is what will be remembered about you and will eventually show up. If you're not doing OK, just say, *"I'm shifting my focus right now and looking to manifest some great opportunities!"*

That will give them no unnecessary information and shut them up. You might say, *"I'm not in the mood to talk about me today, what's up with you?"* The good old change-the-subject routine works well. If you mention, *"I'm great! Things are moving along well right now!"*, then that is what will be remembered. Here's the bottom line: make sure you surround yourself with positive people in your everyday life and especially at work and don't speak negatively about yourself or others to co-workers. People will talk! Don't give them the fuel to use against you.

Now we will explore the people you go out on the road with...Your ROAD PARTNERS....

ROAD PARTNERS

> *"If you wish to know the character of a prince, look at his ministers: if you wish to understand the man, look at his friends."*

--Rabbi Hillel

YOUR FRIENDS ARE A REFLECTION OF YOU!

If you are a man that travels with road partners while attempting to meet women, be aware that women will absolutely check out your friends to get a clear reflection of who you are. In this chapter we will explore how your friends can make or break you while attempting to connect with women. It is very important to go out on the road with people who have a similar vibe to yours, or it may drag you down. My mother always said "You are who you travel with." Some men you hang out with might look good on the outside, but will blow some of your action if they are rude or negative in front of women you're meeting for the first time. Off-handed comments from friends like this can ruin new connections with women.

Are you one of those jokers who puts your friends down all the time? Do you allow your friends to do that to you? Take a stand for yourself and ask them to stop now. Tell them clearly that their negativity isn't helping any of you score with women, and they will listen. Most guys won't tell each other this kind of thing right up front, and so much time and energy is wasted because they aren't honest with each other. So many women — so little time, so why blow it because of your insensitive friend? Share your new plan of shifting your attitude and be the leader in your group. Helping your friends helps your quality of life along the way.

Here's an even better idea: now that you have some new awareness, share this book with other men. Then you can discuss different issues and support each other in a new way.

ROLE MODELS/SUPPORT

Role models are important. If you know people whose lives are living examples of what you desire to achieve, be willing to ask for some assistance and feedback. Most people are happy and honored to offer advice if you sincerely request their support while you're growing. Seeking out their wisdom and letting them know you'd appreciate their guidance and belief in you makes them feel like they can contribute to helping someone else's vision for success. Most successful people enjoy discussing their unique angles and techniques in whatever topic you inquire about. People that are happy in dynamic relationships can enhance your life and open your eyes to discover new ways of creating love in your life. You will be surprised at how many people will be supportive, especially if you have been negative in the past. As you evolve, people will say, *"I'm so glad you've shifted; you used to be so down and depressed."* In time, you will become an inspiration to those observing your changes!

Having friends hold a vision for you and your dreams is very powerful. You must request roadside assistance occasionally. Some men have challenges asking for support. This is similar to the popular mindset in society that when men ask for directions it is not masculine...that belief is not true. Sometimes a little assistance will save you precious time and get you headed in the right direction. Life is too short...Ask and you shall receive support!

ASSEMBLE A PIT CREW

Having a support system will make a big difference. Many men in my seminars have no social or support system and desire to connect with other men to go out with. How can you assemble a pit crew? Go where men go who enjoy similar interests. It is essential to join organizations and groups to meet men to socialize with. Check for men's support groups or sporting leagues in your area. You must let others know you want some company. Check the internet and team up with other single men and women! Share your goals with friends in the same situation and work as a team. Asking for support and keeping your conversations on an up note will help. Join groups! Volunteer! Be a leader!

FRIENDLY WARNING SIGNS AND SUPPORT

When out with friends, build each other up instead of competing with each other. Women are much more turned on by guys that are supportive and show camaraderie instead of competition. It is much more powerful that you are secure enough to build your friends up in front of women and the result is that women will be more willing to open up. Remember to say only things you don't mind having repeated, and be aware that some men can be competitive. Some men do completely change their energy vibe when an attractive woman enters the room, and if it's a powerful sex vibe, it may scare some women away. You can see the metamorphosis occur by observing the tonality change and body language in some men. Women sense this sexual energy and some men may make comments to their friends that turn women off. Keep your comments on an upleveled vibe and give warning signs to your friends if they are sending out vibes that repel. Discuss these issues with your friends and make some agreements to give each other support. Here's how.

Some people aren't aware of the messages they send out, verbally or non-verbally. Give friends permission to give you a signal or a movement of some kind to make you aware when you are spewing negative vibes or being too pushy or arrogant. They might shake their head from side-to-side as if they are saying no or do a thumbs down, or use a subtle zipper signal across the mouth as a signal to shut off the stream of words coming out of your mouth. No one else will know if it is done discreetly. Then you can shift the conversation to project the right energy, to make new friends and perhaps close the deal. Be supportive and assist your friends that need help with this, by bringing up this friendly warning sign system to your road partners. If you need an occasional reminder, ask your friends to give you the signs to change your message and eventually you will catch yourself before the words slip out, therefore changing old habits!

WHO IS DRIVING YOUR MIND?

There are certain situations that can make your mind go into a tailspin. For example: People who go out with exaggerated expectations of meeting someone can occasionally get disappointed if they don't make a connection and their friends do. If you are with a friend one evening who does connect and you don't, be happy for him. Don't mope around or complain, because you may project negative energy and ruin your friend's good time and chase women away. Believe that you will connect sometime soon and don't be attached to when or where. It's normal to feel left out once in awhile, and this is a good time to work on that inner dialogue that may creep into your mind on your way home. Often, this is the time that those negative voices get louder and very negative for some people. This is when you might get negative and tell yourself or a friend, *"I'm sad about being alone. I'm tired of this, I'm sick of dating. I'm afraid I'll never fall in love. I'm frustrated with my situation. I'm giving up on this. Women aren't attracted to me."* Your friends may attempt to bring you out of this mindset, yet it's ultimately up to you to take control of those old beliefs and be kind to yourself. Who is driving your mind? Take control!

DON'T GET FUELED BY WORDS.

Remember, when you constantly speak to yourself or others with negative beliefs, your body corresponds to those beliefs:

Your THOUGHTS = Your WORDS = Your REALITY

Listen to those words: "Sad, tired, sick, afraid, frustrated, giving up." Those are draining words. Didn't they make you feel depressed just reading them? They certainly bring you down when you hear them from a friend or when you say them to yourself. Those down thoughts are currents of energy, powerful currents, and they can cause your body to create discomfort and diseases to correspond to those thoughts (headaches, depression, no dates, no sex, ulcers, chronic fatigue, aches and pains...). If you believe sad thoughts, you'll attract circumstances to make you sad...like a magnet.

I hear that the end of the evening is one of the times that singles are hardest on themselves; others are pairing up while they end up alone. I have mentioned this to people, and they will say, " *Oh, people are such big babies,"* or *"That person would have to be very insecure to feel like that after a party. Grow up."* My extensive research and surveys indicate that, next to breaking up with someone, this is the time (on your way home from a club or party) when singles internally beat themselves up. They feel rejected and if they have been drinking it may intensify their mood. Alcohol is a depressant, so it will definitely contribute to your mood if you're bummed out. Mind-altering drugs, like extacy, speed, and marijuana, can cause depression when they wear off, which adds to the negative mind jam.

If someone is putting out these vibes around you, ask them, *"Can you see how saying and thinking those things makes you feel? Change the channel on that thought."* Let them know you are there to support them to have more empowering beliefs. Suggest some new beliefs they might consider. Tell them your new discovery about how broadcasting negative words creates negative results. You might just change their life!

I hear men (and women) really beat up on each other on the

way out of parties and clubs. They call each other losers and make really nasty, negative comments — which can bum someone out, even if it is done in jest. If you're the person in your group of friends who receives a lot of attention, be sensitive to your friends who may not receive as much that evening. I'm not talking about baby-sitting, just be conscious of their presence. Introduce them to others; include them in your conversations. When the evening is over, be sensitive to them with supportive words instead of energy-draining jokes that can hurt them. Some friends may feel bad enough about not connecting with anyone, without your sarcasm adding to their emotions. Many clients have told me horror stories of comments that friends said to them in jest about being losers (and much worse), and it leaves deep imprints in their minds for years. Become a supportive friend, not a negative influence.

No one is driving your mind but you. On your way home from an event or a nightclub — when your negative beliefs get into the driver's seat — your mind can get out of control. Take back control in the moment, or your mind can race off again.

ROAD-PARTNER COMMUNICATION

When you're going out with friends (male or female) to meet people, I strongly suggest that you talk about how you will handle some of the adventures that await you. What if one of you connects with someone and the other doesn't? Set a time to meet later (say, a half-hour) if you get into a conversation with a person/people at an event. Be clear about where and when you will reconnect, and where you will be if you get separated, especially if it's a big event (concert, festival, or big theaters).

Some people assume that their friends know what actions they prefer and what they would do in certain circumstances. Assume nothing! Some friends just have a flow and let each other mingle with no problem. Others don't like to be separated from you, and if you're an independent type, it can be annoying. Talk about the details and how you will deal with issues honestly! Who's driving? What if one friend wants to leave early? What time will you meet, and where? Do you inform someone in your group you are leaving early or just assume that they will realize you have left? Have some clear conversations about riding together and set up a spot to connect. Don't assume people know what you would do when you are out. Communicate!

If you are drinking, please designate someone to drive that is sober. I have seen too many people get D.U.I.s by not being smart and letting the person that is sober drive. Some people refuse to admit that they drank too much and can get belligerent when they drink. A loud drunken man or women who gets bossy and loud at an event is such a turnoff. If you are drinking, ask someone else to drive or take a taxi!

ASK FRIENDS FOR SUPPORT

If you need support, don't assume your friends know. You need to ask for it! If you aren't able to give yourself support at the time, ask your friends directly! Most people are not mind-readers and will help if you ask them (especially men!). If you are in a down mood, perhaps going to a crowded bar or party isn't the right place to be. Don't force yourself to go out with friends when you aren't in the mood to be in a crowd. If you go out with friends it may snap you out of your mood, yet don't expect their undivided attention at a party or event if they aren't aware of your need for support at the time. Set up a time when you can go to a quiet spot so that you can have your friends' full attention without distractions. Don't expect them to just "*know*" you needed them. *Ask for help!*

While you are setting a new pathway you may need to ask for support along the way. If you don't have friends that can, go to a dating coach like myself or a counselor. You must realize that for a time you may have been so negative that some people won't believe you are shifting gears and taking responsibility for your life all of a sudden. Some of my clients claim that when they tell their friends what they are doing their friends have been very supportive while others just laughed at them saying, "*Sure, we'll see.*" When your

145

friends see you achieve results in your life, they may even follow your example. Watch as you change and set higher standards for yourself, because you may want to let go of your old road partners. You will be up-leveling your life, and they may think you are crazy. Who cares? Do it anyway and ask for support from people in your life that have an open mind and have a more positive outlook on life!

You may also go to a male mentor that you respect and want to emulate. I do not advise soliciting feedback from anyone who is not supportive of your well-being — this could be detrimental to your health. I find it very interesting how many men will take the opinions of bitchy women or angry relatives who can't stand them and who hold on to their opinions for years. Take a look at the lives of the people you ask for support and then decide if you want to heed their advice.

Some people care too much about what others think of them, even though they may say they don't care about others' opinions. Remember, most people are so concerned about what you are thinking of them, they may not be judging you as much as you think they are. They are thinking of themselves most of the time and wondering what you are thinking about them. Relax and let go of others' opinions and as long as you are happy with yourself, who cares what others think about you! It's only an opinion and everyone has one based on their own set of beliefs! Take feedback from people that you highly respect and let the others go! Now let's discuss going out with women friends.

WOMEN ROAD PARTNERS

When you're out with women friends, don't give a mixed signal by hanging on too tightly to your girl "friends," because other women will think you are taken — and they'll think you're slime for flirting with them. Some women are more attracted when they see you in the company of another interesting woman (or women) and the air of mystery is created. Use this mystery wisely since it can backfire on you if you send the wrong message. When you are out with a woman, or a group of them, the other women are watching how you act with them to see if you're taken. Being overly affectionate and snuggly with girl "friends" can send mixed signals. Sometimes in a group situation, female friends can get a little possessive or protective of you and will chase other women away.

Be honest with your women buddies about your boundaries and ask them to help you meet women if you're shy. Have your women friends casually mention to the single women that you want to meet them. I have often initiated connections with my men friends and it helps to break the ice.

Women friends can also sense if the woman you are checking out is interested in you. Women have extra sensory perception and can easily pick up signals from other women to know if they have their eyes set on you. I have been out with many men who misread signals. Ask your women friends to give you their reading on a woman that you are interested in. If you are not sure of a signal, flirt anyway. It is good to practice as often as possible.

Remember to tell your women friends what you are looking for in a mate and that you want to have them help you find a women to have a relationship with! Then when you are out, match your actions and your words with your requests! Ask for their feedback from observing you while you are out. They may be able to give you some insights on things you may say or do unconsciously when you are flirting with women. You may discover that your women road partners are one of your best assets to gaining new insights about yourself, the image you project and assisting you when out on the town looking for love.

Next is the road partner checklist that is designed to have you take a look at your traveling partners. Ask these simple questions of yourself to see if you might need to make a few adjustments.

ROAD-PARTNER CHECKLIST
LIST THE PEOPLE IN YOUR LIFE NOW.

♦ *Do your friends have similar energy? Complimentary energy?*

♦ *Do you have energy enhancing or energy draining friends?*

♦ *Do they have lives you admire and want to emulate?*

♦ *Are they supporting you in your relationship goals and life goals?*

♦ *Are you supportive of each other in whatever phase you're in?*

♦ *Are you in social situations that support your life goals?*

♦ *Can you have open, honest conversations and ask for support from your friends?*

♦ *How do you treat women when you are out on the town with your friends?*

♦ *Are you a good friend to others?*

♦ *What are the qualities you look for in a friend?*

♦ *Could you expand your circle of friends?*

♦ *What actions are you taking to make new friends?*

♦ *What actions will you take now to make this happen?*

Building and maintaining friendships, socializing and networking, takes time, focus and energy. You must have the stamina and energy to do all these extra activities. In the next chapter you will learn some new ways to fire up your energy and spark your performance, so you will be energized to meet someone anytime anywhere! Let's rev up those engines...

DAILY TUNE-UPS

"Energy and persistence conquer all things."

--Benjamin Franklin

ARE YOU READY FOR MAXIMUM PERFORMANCE?

We will now be covering many energy tips to assist you in achieving your daily life goals while out on the road.

We all have different energy at different times and phases of our lives, especially in the phase we call "single life." Our energy and vitality goes up and down. When it's down, what steps can we take to retrieve it and achieve maximum performance? Do you need a physical tune-up?

As we age, some of us lose some of our youthful vitality; there is wear and tear on the vehicle known as our body. Even when you're young, your party schedule can wear you out! You must maintain balance for maximum performance.

WHAT IS FUELING YOU?

Your diet contributes to your glucose levels and influences your moods. The foods and liquids you consume are the fuel for your body. According to the widely renowned Dr. Tobin Watkinson, it is challenging to maintain high energy with all the chemical additives we have in our foods and drinks. Using artificial sweeteners, diet soda and sugar based food decreases brain function and alters the glucose levels in the body, which causes fatigue and brain fog, depending on body chemistry. Different foods and chemicals, electronic devices, air and water will bring about unique symptoms in each individual. If we are nutritionally unbalanced, we don't function with all our energy. Being single takes a lot of extra energy, and if your diet is poor, you won't have that extra zip to get out in the game with a full tank.

We must rejuvenate our cellular structure all the time by being aware of what we take into our minds and our bodies, and controlling our environments. We have available to us healing body treatments (massage, accupuncture...), simple remedies, naps, and exercises to keep our bodies in tip-top shape. With the latest technologies, we can retard and reverse the aging process and keep our energy in balance. We will be exploring all of the experts in more detail in one of my books in this series.

According to Dr. Chein, the grandfather of anti-aging, the natural aging process slows down our metabolism, our brain function, and greatly affects our hormone levels and energy. In his book *Age Reversal,* he writes that these hormone levels can safely be replaced by first testing your hormones, then naturally bringing them into balance with natural products on the market today.

Another alternative is to do a Live Blood Cell Analysis which is an intimate look at the inside environment of your body. Is your blood a clean clear lake or a stagnant swamp? A single drop of blood examined under a high-powered microscope can reveal nutritional deficiencies, the activity of your immune system and the overall state of your health. Dr. William Thorton and Dr. Deborah Medoff believe that Live Cell Analysis is the inside story of your body's tendency toward health or disease, sometimes long before you're even aware of a problem, so you can take preventive measures. Since anti-aging and nutrition is a part of my life style, I went to check my blood and was amazed at the results. Even the water you drink affects your acid and akaline balance. Why not take a look inside your internal system and discover why your energy might be low.

Many people over thirty wonder why they don't have the same zip in their step as before and have no drive to keep going. Nutritional supplements and natural hormone replacements will tune you up fast to prepare your vehicle for love and hot, passionate sex. Without the energy, who has the desire to perform and fire-up your lover (if you can even attract one)? Get checked by a hormone or anti-aging specialist in your area. It is not advised to go on natural hormone replacements without the proper testing first.

Before going out to connect, make sure you eat something so your energy is up and your blood sugar is normalized (so you won't get shaky from not eating all day). Many people go all day on coffee and donuts and wonder why they feel blue. Eating heavy carbs or sugars can make you sleepy and not as sharp mentally. Eat a healthy snack before going out (nuts, a piece of fruit, an ounce of cheese, half of an energy bar) and you will maintain a higher level of energy until you have your next meal. Then if you have a before-dinner cocktail, the alcohol won't affect you as much as on an empty stomach. You will be able to communicate the right vibes and make a good impression. I eat 5-6 small meals a day to maintain my balance. Not eating all day because you're going to dinner is not an action plan, if you want to be your best.

The diet system that I follow, THE ZONE™, actually will deliver prepared food to your home or office with the snacks included. For the busy businessman, this is an easy way to eat well without having to prepare your own food. All meals are balanced and in perfect proportions to maintain your weight and get in top running condition. I have information about prepared food delivery services on my website.

This diet system may not be for everyone and I'm only mentioning it because for busy, active people, it keeps your blood sugar levels even and energy up. Whether you're a vegetarian or have special diet restrictions, eating small meals all day works for most people who need extra energy. Your car can't run without fuel, so how do you expect your body to run on empty?

Your water intake also affects your moods and energy. Lack of water is the number one trigger of daytime fatigue and by drinking 8-10 glasses a day it can ease back and joint pain . Water keeps the system hydrated and 75% of Americans are chronically dehydrated. Drink more water and you will find that you will be able to focus more clearly, have a sharper memory and nicer skin.

Here are more energy tips to keep your engines running. You may have heard these tips before, but have you tried them? Remember: just a change in your physical state can shift you into a higher gear and give you that extra zip and energy you need to stay in balance.

ENERGY HABITS FOR EVERYDAY

When your energy levels are low, there are many simple energy exercises and activities you can do to counteract these conditions. Get into the habit of taking energy breaks several times a day and check in with yourself. Give some of these tips a try!

♦ *Stop and do deep-breathing exercises. Breathe in to the count of 8. Hold the breath for the count of 4. Exhale slowly to the count of 8. Repeat 10 times.*

♦ *Leave your environment for 10-15 minutes. Move your body with your arms swinging freely – opposite arms and legs called "heterolateral walking." (left arm swings forward with the rigt leg)*

♦ *Play a theme song that gets you going while getting ready and on your way to your destination.*

♦ *Take a stretching break. If you have a yard and the weather permits, go outside. Breathe.*

♦ *Take a catnap in your car or office if you can't make it home to freshen up. If you are near the ocean or water, take a blanket for a 15-minute pick-me-up nap.*

♦ *Turn off everything (phones, pagers, computers, TV, radio* and listen to the stillness).

♦ Do a simple kinesiology exercise called "cross-crawling," which is touching your elbows or hands to opposite knee or foot while standing, for up to 2 minutes. This movement causes a balance between the right- and left-brain hemispheres, facilitates learning, reduces stress, and opens our creative centers and can be done almost anywhere.

♦ Eat a snack! Keep raw nuts or almond/peanut butter (a source of protein) and fruit around for in-between pick-me-ups. Keeping your blood sugar up is vital to maintaining energy.

♦ Put on your favorite clothes that make you feel lucky, handsome and powerful (if you don't have any, it's time to go shopping).

♦ The thymus gland is the first organ to be affected by stress and is the seat of our life energy, so it is thought of as the link between mind and body. Thymus tapping is very helpful, and you will feel it immediately. The thymus gland lies beneath the upper part of the breastbone in the middle of the chest, and lightly tapping it for 30 – 60 seconds can increase the activity of the gland and strengthen the immune mechanisms. The thymus gland monitors and regulates energy flow through the body and energy systems. When the thymus gland is weak or underactive, your life energy will be lowered, and the tapping exercises and techniques will activate the thymus — bringing it into balance. Your physical environment, social relationships, your posture and the food you ingest influence the thymus. I personally have had amazing results with this tapping technique and wanted to share this energy secret with all of you.

♦ Splash cold water on your face and brush your teeth. (Carry a tune-up kit, a small bag of supplies, including your toothbrush and toothpaste and/or mouthwash, dental floss, a regular or electric razor (if you have a rough beard), hairbrush/comb and hair gel/spray, if needed, cologne, condoms (just in case), hand lotion and moisturizer for your skin with SPF. You'll be prepared for action and looking good!

♦ Clap for 30-60 seconds in your car on your way to your destination as if you're enjoying a good play or concert. Give yourself an ovation.

♦ Read true-life, inspirational stories from books, such as "Small Miracles", "Don't Sweat the Small Stuff...in Love", "Chicken Soup for the Soul", any of Wayne Dyer's or Nathaniel Brandon's books. Ask your women friends for some suggestions.

♦ Sing at home, in the car, at work.

♦ Use the NLP technique called anchoring, which utilizes going back to a memory where you felt vital and invigorated from an activity. Feel, see, smell, hear, and experience all of the sensations you felt while doing that activity in every inch of your body. Use your senses and experience it all over again in vivid detail. Touch your body in a spot over and over (squeeze your wrist or tap on your heart, slap your knee). This works like magic before a date or business presentation to reinvent that inner feeling of success and energy.

♦ Use one of my favorite Bach Flower™ products called "Rescue Remedy™" which calms you down and helps you focus and clears your mind. You can get it at most health food stores. It is great before a hot date, an important meeting or before going out to meet new people. Other Bach Flower Remedies can help with all the different emotions that we face in the dating process. You can get information at your local health food store on these amazing products.

♦ Read a motivational book/quote that inspires you.

♦ Take the stairs instead of the elevator at work or a nearby building to get your heart pumping on your way to meetings.

♦ Self-hypnosis: Start at the top of your head and relax each muscle, talking softly in your mind or out loud, filling each muscle and nerve with new vital energy. Contract and relax each muscle (hold it for a count of 6 and then let it relax). Continue down the body until you reach your toes. It takes about 10-15 minutes, and you will feel rejuvenated. Your body will respond if you tell it to. I promise.

♦ Buy hypnosis tapes on energy and relaxation.

♦ Listen to soothing music while doing breathing exercises.

♦ Take an invigorating shower and scrub your body with a loofah sponge.

♦ Look at a photo of art/landscape/sunrise/mountains/beauties of nature that you enjoy, get a small (postcard size) work of art that sends you to a peaceful place and keep it at work.

♦ Move your body everyday or at least 3 times a week outside, if possible. This means a walk/run/bike in a park, beach, woods or any place in nature.

♦ Take a jacuzzi.

♦ Go for a short drive.

♦ Get into a bath filled with warm water. Lie back and put your ears under the water. Listen to your own breath for 10 minutes. As you let the water go down the drain imagine your stress going down the drain with the water.

♦ Meditate to focus your mind. Use a mantra or group of words such as "Peace," "Be still," or the sound "AHHHH" or "OOOMMM" over and over. There are many books and unique meditation techniques for you to experiment with, and they work when you practice them.

♦ Get into gratitude about your strengths and blessings when your stress level goes up.

♦ Call someone you love and say hello.

♦ Ask for support!

♦ Talk to yourself about how much fun you are having until the fun shows up.

♦ Do what many women do — buy yourself something!

♦ Go get a balancing massage or foot reflexology treatment by a professional massage therapist to help you relax before a big night out. Getting touched helps with built up sexual frustration!

♦ Say a heartfelt prayer for yourself knowing your prayers are answered. See the desired outcome in your mind and feel it in your soul. Prayer works!

♦ Remind yourself of 7 blessings each day.

♦ Coffee and caffeine drinks will give you a buzz and pump your adrenals. The caffeine habit is easy for people to fall into when they need that extra kick to their engine, but coffee isn't really the best choice, because it makes some people hyper, it greatly affects the way your breath smells and it dehydrates your system. So beware. Try herbal tea or natural stimulants if you are concerned about caffeine.

♦ Many people drink alcohol to relax. If you choose to drink, eat *something before and during drinking and drink lots of water before bedtime and in between drinks. Taking some B-complex vitamins and aspirin before and after has been known to prevent hangovers. There are also homeopathic remedies for hangovers that really work! Check your local health food store.*

Now let's take a look at some environmental energy drainers and how we can make adjustments to keep our energy up!

ENERGY DRAINERS IN YOUR ENVIRONMENT
- *Florescent lights*
- *Computers*
- *Electric heat and blankets*
- *Digital phones/pagers*
- *Air quality*

Cellular phones and pagers worn on your body can deplete your energy. Many people are affected by electromagnetic fields, and the frequencies from them can put you out of balance. How do we get our balance back? Don't wear pagers on your body or hold your cell phone close to your ear. Buy a small headset to keep the batteries away from your brain. Some people experience an increase in energy when they follow this advice.

Electronic equipment and microwaves send out "currents", and operate at frequencies that some people are extremely sensitive to. Electric heaters, electric blankets, heating pads and computers can also set you off balance. The organs that get affected are the pineal and thymus glands, and they sometimes need extra support with nutritional supplementation. By using a protective screen for your computer, you can prevent a drain on your energy.

Bright lights and fluorescent lights at offices might be changed to softer (or full spectrum) lighting. Unnatural lighting and different colors of light in a room can affect your energy also. Light, color, and sound therapies are used to increase the energy flow in our systems. There are specialists in these fields across the nation.

The air quality where you work and live is vital. Open windows for cross-ventilation, or if there are no windows, buy an air purifier/ionizer to clean out the dust and mold. When the air smells clean and crisp it helps you to think more clearly. Using aromatherapy dispensers will also aid in creating an environment that supports your energy. Most health food stores carry a nice variety and they make your office or home smell great!

Besides all of the above tune-ups, here are some energy-producing thoughts about single life that you can contemplate before going out. Implant positive emotions, thoughts, and impressions in your subconscious mind to affect your outcomes before going out on dates or looking to connect. Remember that our subconscious mind takes things literally, and it responds to feelings and repetition. The subconscious takes thing personally, is alert and functioning at all times and receives direct messages from our conscious mind. Choose your thoughts carefully! The consciousness of love precedes the actual manifestation of it. *"ACT AS IF"* before the event, and it will show up eventually.

TUNE-UP YOUR THOUGHTS
ENERGY-PRODUCING THOUGHTS & PHRASES:

The things you say to yourself before you go out are very, very important. *YOU HAVE THE POWER!* Set new intentions for yourself! Take control of your thoughts!

- *I meet incredible people wherever I go.*
- *I'm happier with life and myself each passing day.*
- *I am an awesome person and attract people that treat me well.*
- *I only attract great people into my life now.*
- *I accept my body, and I feel good about myself.*
- *I attract people who love me just the way I am.*
- *I am clear on what I want in a relationship and that person is seeking me now!*
- *I know that I deserve love from a available mate.*

159

- *I am attracting work that is fulfilling to my heart and abilities.*
- *I attract a mate that is faithful and trustworthy.*
- *I trust love and am attracting people everywhere I go.*
- *I listen to my instinctive body signals and am always internally guided to the perfect people, situations, and circumstances on my path to love.*
- *Women are wonderful, and I attract a woman that wants a monogamous relationship with me.*
- *I am open to love all around me now!*
- *I am open to meeting new, interesting people.*
- *I attract interesting people, opportunities, and relationships into my life now.*
- *I believe in myself.*
- *There is someone for me to love that is ready, available, and open to my love, and I am attracting her now!*
- *I am on a new path to connecting what works in all areas of my life!*
- *I am a fun-loving person and have friends that support me.*
- *I have a great partner who loves me just as I am.*
- *I am a Gift to the people in my life!*
- *I make smart choices in all my relationships!*
- *I attract fun, energetic friends and increase my social structure.*
- *I am open to new experiences everyday that lead me to my mate!*
- *I am grateful for all my blessings and talents.*
- *I am responsible for creating solid relationships in my life.*
- *I open my energy to project confidence.*

You can feel the difference using these type of statements on a regular basis. You must feel and believe that you are a benefit to someone before you can actually attract someone. Write it down and say out loud: *"I am a gift."* When you come to know that you are a gift, then you will start attracting people who are at a new, fresh level and never go back to the old you. It's a new way to think about yourself — we are all gifts! We all have love and experiences to share. That's why we're here. Your heart wants to give to someone. Your soul wants to merge with some-one. Your body wants to make love, be passionate and connect with someone. How will that feel to you? Can you envision that experience for yourself now before love shows up? You must integrate the emotions, pictures, sounds, tastes, and smells of the experience before it shows up. Many of the top athletes practice this visualization technique and control their thoughts before a game to succeed. Whether it is baseball, golf, basketball, foot-ball, hockey...you name the sport, and you can bet that the top athletes in each field practice similar techniques.

Attracting women is no different than a sport in creating a great rapport with yourself and women. Seeing and feeling the successful results *BEFORE* you play in the game is vital. Re-member to tune-up your energy before you connect. Be your own motivational coach! These techniques can add that extra spark it takes to magnetize women!

Let's move ahead to discover new powerful tools to create rapport with others by learning their unique communication styles. You'll also discover techniques that will cure the rejection factor and increase your social structure...

PART THREE
ON THE ROAD TO SUCCESS

OUT ON THE ROAD

11

"Life is either a daring adventure or nothing."

—Helen Keller

POWER-CHARGED CONNECTIONS

So, here you are, taking good care of yourself, feeling better about how you look, talking positively to others — and to ol' number one! Now, it's time to go out and connect! When you go out, in general, some people are not that open or kind, and some can be downright rude. To build power-charged connections you must connect with others that are on your same vibe. It's all about connecting in general to humans, not just women you are physically drawn toward. Notice other people's energy. Get in tune with others' vibes. Open up your ears, eyes and senses to connect with more people, and become aware and listen to what is happening all around you.

You will now learn how to have power-charged connections by introducing you to the three basic communication models that are used in Neuro Linguistic Programming. NLP is the science of using your brain, your language, and your behavior to achieve your desired result. By learning how people communicate and connect, you will be able to read the energy of people easier and elicit the words and phrases to create deeper feelings of connection.

COMMUNICATION STYLES

Based on the NLP Model, the three basic communication styles are auditory, kinesthetic and visual. Knowing a person's primary style of communication is especially vital in your first meeting. When you're trying to establish rapport, listen to the way people talk, their eye movements and body language signals. This will help you become more aware of their most prominent connecting style.

Following each of the NLP descriptions are words and phrases most often associated with that particular style of communication. Listen for these words and phrases to discover the primary communication style of those around you and to see if you are compatible. You do not need to have the same communication style to have success with people. Becoming aware of how to communicate effectively will provide you with powerful tools to connect and build rapport with anyone anywhere. Remember: we can powerfully influence others and win their hearts by knowing how their minds operate.

BUILDING RAPPORT

Building a safe connection first is essential with women. To establish this safe feeling, matching and mirroring a person's behavior when you connect the first time establishes instant rapport in most cases. This is where becoming aware of body language and energy works to make a connection. When you first meet someone, using matching means to match actions with the same side (their left with your left). Mirroring is when you match them like looking in a mirror (their left with your right). This will assist the person to accept your ideas and suggestions more readily.

Matching their physiology, which is fifty-five percent of the connection, includes copying :
- *a person's posture*
- *the way they sit*
- *their facial expressions*
- *eye contact and movements*
- *hand movements and gestures (subtly)*

This will make them feel like they have known you forever. When you blink and breathe the way they do, it works wonders to build rapport and easy communication. Be subtle while doing this otherwise it can have the opposite effect, and the other person will not trust you.

When you first meet someone, you greet them and then become aware of and match:

- *the tonality of their voice*
- *the speed of their words*
- *the volume and the timbre or quality of their speaking*
- *the inflections and pauses.*

Then, becoming a good listener will give you the magic keys to the person's primary communication style which will provide you with the tools to win their affections.

Watching a person's eye patterns while asking them questions will expose their primary communication style. When you ask questions, notice if the person looks up while answering and you will establish that they are visually remembering. Another person will look from side to side or tilt their head sideways when listening, establishing that they are an auditory-based communicator. The Kinesthetic Person will look down and to the right while connecting to answers. Below are more distinctions to assist you in understanding the most common traits of each communication style, providing you with more powerful communication tools.

THE AUDITORY PERSON

Auditories are sound-based people, usually engaged in sales-related activities or people-oriented businesses (attorneys, singers, musicians, public speakers, radio and TV hosts). They listen to how you say things, not to what you show them. They prefer listening to music to watching television or videos.

When they are in auditory access, they tilt their heads slightly, with side-to-side eye movements. They will remember what people said and how they said it. They are sensitive to the "tones" people use when speaking to them.

They talk on the phone a lot and prefer verbal communication to letters or online communication. If you're in a relationship with an auditory person — or just starting one — they want to hear from you. Just calling to say "*Hello*," will make them happy. They love romantic chats and want you to share your thoughts out loud.

Many women are auditory and will comment that their boyfriends don't call often enough for them to feel connected. The auditory person doesn't need to see you as often as the others do, but hearing from you can make their day.

This goes for any auditory people in your life — friends, lovers, family members; calling them often to check in and let them know you are thinking of them works wonders.

In conversations, you will hear them say things such as: *"I heard that you were there." "That sounds terrific!" "That rings true for me." "His voice totally turned me on."* So, if you want to persuade them, say things like: *"Doesn't that movie sound great?" "That sounds like so much fun — perhaps we could go there together."* Draw their attention to how things sound. Describe dates with sound based words like: *"A nice quiet evening listening to romantic music. How does that sound to you?"* It works.

Auditory people are turned on by gifts that are sound related, such as concert tickets, CDs, musical boxes, nature sound machines, wind chimes, and they love romantic background music while dining out. Creating an environment with sound is very important. They may leave a place because it is too loud. Before planning a concert evening, it's a good idea to ask your date about her musical tastes — especially if she's an auditory — because bringing her to a heavy metal rock concert may not be her thing.

When you promise something to an auditory person, make sure you follow up on it. Your word is very important. Finally, remembering what they told you is a winning formula to build trust with an auditory person.

WORDS AND PHRASES YOU MAY HEAR
FROM AN AUDITORY:

"I heard," "sounds like," "rings a bell," "listen," "attune," "I'll be all ears," "tune in/out," "I was speechless," "outspoken," "tell me more," "resonate," "harmonizes," "I question that," "I hear that," "silence," "overtones."

THE KINESTHETIC PERSON

Kinesthetic people make decisions by how they feel, rather than by what they see or hear. They process information mostly from touch, feelings, gut instincts, hunches and emotions. They have to "feel it" before they trust you. If they feel good about you, they will open up.

Kinesthetic people talk about feelings. *"I felt so excited yesterday when we had our discussion," "That makes me feel so stressed out when…," "I have to get a grip," "Let's touch base," "That rubs me the wrong way," "I had a gut feeling about that."*

They tend to look down when accessing their feelings, sometimes placing their hands over their abdomens or their hearts or the midlines of their bodies (body language clues). Their vocal tones are lower and deeper while accessing emotions kinesthetically.

If you desire to connect with and persuade a Kinesthetic Person, ask them how they feel about things. Direct their attention to how things feel, and it will make them feel good about you. When you get the clear signals that a kinesthetic woman is interested, you may want to touch her gently on the shoulder, hand, or arm to warm her up to you. If she is wearing soft clothing (which kinesthetics usually do), touch her arm gently and rub while saying, *"You feel soooo soft." "You body feels so good against me."*

When a kinesthetic woman is attracted to you, she will love that you notice details and tell her how you feel about whatever it might be (her hair, her clothing, her skin). Of course, if she isn't interested, you will definitely know by how she responds. If she moves away or crosses her arms, she doesn't feel safe. When a kinesthetic feels secure around you, she becomes like a kitten, and can melt into your touch if you're on the same vibration. You can rub her and hold her to make her feel loved.

Warm, caring hugs are sure signs of kinesthetic people — they love receiving them just as much as giving them. Hugging, petting and kissing gently, yet passionately, are primary keys to a romantic interlude with a kinesthetic. Being too pushy has the opposite effect.

Kinesthetic people love gifts like massages, facials, manicures (as do most women), good food, bath gels and beads, soft-fabric clothing (silk or cashmere), chocolates, flowers, soft bedding or blankets, and soft, fluffy things (lingerie, hosiery). When you see your kinesthetic woman, hug her and tell her that you're so happy to feel her in your arms. You might say it sounds corny, yet it works with kinesthetic women

WORDS AND PHRASES YOU MAY HEAR
FROM A KINESTHETIC:

"What do you feel?" "I felt so connected" "get a hold of," "that touched me," "tap into," "let's make contact," "feeling," "I handled it," "don't put pressure on me," "that upset me," "concrete," "I have to grasp it," " I'll handle it," " You'll catch on."

THE VISUAL PERSON

The visual person understands what you say by what they can see. Like Viewmasters™, visuals make decisions by how they see things in their minds. They are sometimes better with faces than names. They are the happiest when you paint pictures in their mind for them: *"I can see us standing on the mountaintop overlooking the beautiful countryside." "I remember the look on your face when we surprised you last week."* They make judgments on appearances and have great visual memories. They pay attention to details and buy things by the way they look. They may be distracted if your shirt is crooked or you have a hair out of place.

When accessing information, visuals will look up, squint, or close their eyes to recall images. They may blink a lot and/or have rapid eye movements when their eyes are closed.

Visuals will sometimes be interior designers, architects, painters, engineers, and clothing designers. They love window-shopping, collecting lots of different items, and beautiful things.

When you buy gifts for a visual person, wrap the gifts tastefully in their favorite color. Flowers, photo frames, albums, and home accessories to match their décor make great gifts. You can make a visual happy by taking them to restaurants with spectacular views, art museums, sight-seeing tours, fashion shows and fireworks displays.

WORDS AND PHRASES YOU MAY HEAR
FROM A VISUAL PERSON

"It looks to me that," "she appears to be," "it dawned on me," "I see it in another way," "my view on it is," "it was revealed to me," I envisioned," "I'm focused on," "I can only imagine," "it was sparkling," "see how clear it was," "show me how it works," "illuminate," "hazy," "bright," "foggy."

One of the biggest challenges in clear communication is listening, and now that you have these powerful communication tools, you will be more successful in communicating with women and everyone that is in your life. Using your ears and really hearing will make you a man that people want to be with in all kinds of relationships. Before using these powerful skills, practice on people everywhere you go and see how easy it is to connect deeper to others. Then practice your new magic with women that you are interested in. Learning effective communication takes time and practice. Make good listening a daily practice and you will see amazing results. Now we will move on to my favorite philosophy of all, one that I live by and that will change your life!

FLIRTING WITH LIFE! ™

One of the greatest things you can do to open up is what I call *FLIRTING WITH LIFE* ™! — especially if you are shy or just getting back out there. This is a great way to build confidence — practice *FLIRTING WITH LIFE* ™! wherever you are and with whomever shows up on your path. I'm not suggesting that you attempt to pick up everyone…just keep your energy open, have fun and notice people. By that I mean normal everyday humanoids! Compliment them with a genuine interest and ask questions that illicit a response beyond "yes" or "no" answers. Be curious and open. I have met the most interesting people this way.

Be nice to everyone you meet — the old lady walking across the street, the mail man, the 7-Eleven counter person, the valet… everybody! Open up your energy with everyday people, practice talking to strangers: *"How are you today?" "I like your hat." "How about that new reality TV show? Do you like it?"*

Don't just talk with people you are interested in meeting, especially if you're just getting back out into the world of new friends. Open yourself up and get used to talking to people with kindness wherever you are. Notice people's activities at all the locations you visit during a day and show interest. I'm talking about the local stores, the printers, the post office, the bank, the dry cleaner…. Sincerely compliment people and remember the names of the people who work behind the counters. If they're not wearing name-tags, ask them their names.

I do this with almost everyone who does any kind of service or work for me, so I always get great service, and most importantly, I influence their day. It is heartwarming to know I have cheered up a person's life experience. It makes me feel connected to people, to life, and it helps to heal some of the sadness I see in strangers' eyes. Wherever you are, people will remember you as an open, kind person and notice you. Especially women! Send out the loving "vibe," and I promise, you will eventually get it back in return.

When you get results, you will think back on reading this, and you will know what I'm talking about and incorporate *"FLIRTING*

WITH LIFE"™ into your daily life. It is magical how it works, and it is so simple.

When you are attending an event (e.g, a company party), or when you walk into a situation where you are uncomfortable, listen to what's taking place. Listen to what people are talking about. You can then include yourself in the conversations. Remember to listen for clues on the specific communication style that someone uses by remembering the words they use most. This will be one of the keys to strengthen your conversation skills. When you are interested in a conversation, add genuine comments to let people know that you are really interested in what they are saying. Repeat them and say something like, "*I heard you mention the play/ show/ event (use the topic) at the pier. It sounds like it was incredible. Where is it located? What was your favorite part?*" Get the person talking. Don't ask questions that make them answer "*yes*" or "*no*." If they're interested, they will continue telling you details, and if not, *NEXT!*

Here is an example of how I met my friend Michael in a common everyday situation with my *FLIRTING WITH LIFE!* ™ technique. On my birthday a few years back, my car broke down. I was meeting my girlfriend (also named Renee) for tea at a nearby spot on the famous Third Street Promenade in Santa Monica. I rode my bike there and waited for my friend in front of the coffee shop. As I waited I was enjoying the warm sun on my face and listening to some music in the background. I was seated in the center of 10 small tables, when I overheard (being the auditory person that I am) someone say "Happy Birthday, John." I turned to see two homeless men dressed in tattered clothing who both needed a shower desperately. One man was giving birthday wishes and a card to a very old homeless man.

Someone else was celebrating being born, so I decided to wish him a happy day and perhaps buy him a cup of coffee. I said in a cheerful voice, *"Happy Birthday to you, it is my birthday too. How about a cup of coffee? My treat!"* He said, *"Sure and Happy Birthday"* in return and I happily delivered his coffee. Then to my surprise an attractive man sitting in front of me turned around and acknowledged my birthday, and asked me if I had a birthday wish. I replied, *"My wish would be to get my car to start and find out why it is over-heating. I had to ride my bike here to meet my girlfriend and left my car on the street."* He said, *"Well, I'm a car mechanic, and I would be happy to give you your wish today and check out your car."* What a miracle! If I hadn't said a word to the homeless man I would have never connected with my new friend.

Obviously, I was thrilled. After chatting for a few more minutes, I told him about my *Love Mechanics* seminars for men, and he was excited to attend the next one since he was recently separated from his wife and was a bit "rusty" in the dating scene. As we went to fix my car we discussed many topics and our friendship began. That was some time ago. Today, Michael is a completely different person. Eventually, he changed careers, from being a car mechanic to being a "Body Mechanic" (a professional massage therapist). He makes four times the amount of money compared to what he earned before. He did a complete "tune-up" on his body, his home environment, his internal work, and now his life is filled with excitement, success, and he is dating beautiful, sensual women like never before.

Michael is thrilled, and I have a friend for life from just saying, *"Happy Birthday"* to a stranger. You never know what magic will happen until you open your mouth and listen to what is happening around you!

Many people are so busy worrying about what they're going to say next instead of listening. If you ask a person to repeat what you just said, many people couldn't remember if you paid them. They were not listening! If I'm with a friend and I think they have stopped listening, I will say, *"Hello. . . what was I just talking about? I didn't think I was that boring."* Then I laugh to break the shock. This is the good old pattern-interrupt technique to shift out of a mood or situation. A change in voice tonality, a sharp movement or sudden noise will take them by surprise and brings them out of their daze into the moment. We are all guilty of this occasionally, and it is important to be aware that this experience can be insulting to others when they know you're not present with them. When you're out meeting new people and you end up chatting with a person that bores you...move on!

Be brave! Talk to those people who interest you. If you get a feeling of rejection, move on, *RISK* and go talk to someone else. In many cases, it's up to the man to create the initial connection. This is the guidance given to women in many of the dating books out in the market. Many books state *"The man must approach first or he isn't a man"*. This is *not* my belief at all, nor is it a true statement, yet many women are waiting and expecting you to make the first move.

How do you know if she is interested? Believe me, women send signals, but too often men just don't get the hint. We want you to be strong and tuned into us. *Look for the signs...listen...hear... us...remember...notice.* We spend time preparing ourselves to look nice, so notice our detailing! Be intoxicated with our eyes...our scent...our lips...skin...hair. Express how you feel in the moment with sincerity (and no heavy sex vibes), and if there is a connection you'll get a strong signal from a woman that is interested.

We enjoy compliments and we want to be appreciated for our beauty, as you do for your accomplishments. All women have something beautiful about them...just compliment us with sincerity; connect and you will have women fawning over you...appreciating you for noticing. In the love game, it's all about numbers, so you must get out there and enjoy your life and connect with people and communicate clearly about what you want, and eventually love (in some form) will show up.

How will you know a woman is interested in you? What are the signs to look for? These are the clear signs that women told me they use to express interest in a man. Many women claim that men just don't see these signs clearly! How many times have you seen signs and walked away and fantasized all week about the girl you "could have met?" Wake up guys! Looks for the signs!

CLEAR "GREEN LIGHT" SIGNALS
A WOMAN WHO <u>IS</u> INTERESTED WILL:

- Smile a lot
- Look away then back again
- Giggle and look away
- Get red in the face
- Play with her hair
- Be near you at the office a lot (the coffee machine, the printer)
- Walk by you 10 times at a club or restaurant
- Like clockwork, walk her dog exactly when you do
- Show up at a bar she knows you go to regularly
- Ask others about you
- Smile and say, "good morning" at the coffee shop you go to everyday
- Bat her eyes at you
- Regularly stand near you at kickboxing class
- Go to the ladies' room 5 times during dinner — passing your table and shyly smiling
- Stare at you from across a room for more than 5 minutes
- Check you out, then turn to a friend and laugh, then turn back to glance at you again
- Point at you and wave directly
- Tilt her head and twist her hair while glancing over at you
- Have open body language
- Cross and uncross her legs and bounce her foot up and down while smiling at you.
- Take off her shoe and swing it seductively on her toes.
- Be downright seductive with her body parts
- Flash you
- Be direct and come onto you
- Touch you a lot during conversation
- Lean in close to you
- Hold her stomach in, her shoulders back, and breasts out so you will notice
- In line at a store commenting, "I wonder what is taking so long?" or "You look like a healthy eater.

174

The woman of your dreams is not going to just crawl into your bed or just walk up to you and say she wants to take you home. Women are constantly saying, *"Where are all the great guys?" or "The men are such wimps! What are they afraid of? I wish they would have more guts to approach me."*

I know some women can make it challenging for you guys, and the truth is one day one woman will say *YES*. So keep on approaching. Remember those numbers and stay unattached!

Most single guys come home after work and think, *Well, I should go to a class/workout/go to a lecture/go out to dinner, but I'm tired and the ball game is on, so I'll stay home tonight.* All those "should've," "could've," "buts," and "someday I'll " get you nowhere. Get off your butt and go out more: take a cooking class, go to a jazz club, book signing, volunteer for a charity event, work out at a new gym, go read a book at a coffee shop, break your habits. On the weekend, there's hiking, biking, cocktails, churches, synagogues, dance clubs. . . the list is endless. Unless you are in a phase where you really need nurturing, do not stay in your apartment (or at home) every night. Magic will happen when you go out! Magic will not happen when you stay in or when you don't connect with others while you're out.

There are so many things to do and so many places to meet available women that want to be loved. Everywhere I go, I hear women say *"Where are the men? There are no good guys, they're all taken."* Women are feeling the same way you are. And you may not think that we want love, sex, passion, and all of the things you want...we absolutely desire all those things and more! And we want you to come in a confident package. So, if you're not feeling confident, start working on it and get support if you want to make it easier. Get a coach to help you keep on your toes. You can book a session with me online or over the phone. Get results!! No excuses!

From my research, I have discovered that if some men experience one or two rejections, they don't want to risk again, especially the shy types. You must realize that some of the women you are approaching may be married, engaged, breaking up — they might be going through the same thing you're going through. They may, or may not, be available to you or anyone at this time. It is not personal! Move on!

You might approach a woman and say, *"You look beautiful today. May I join you for a cup of coffee?"* She might say, *"No, thank you"* in a rude tone of voice, and men sometimes feel stabbed in the heart. You might go to lunch and see someone eating alone and say, *"Are you having lunch by yourself? Would you mind if I join you?"* She might say, *"No,"* and you think she was kind of a bitch. That may not mean she's not attracted to you — it could mean she just got her period, or she's having a bad day, or she had a fight with her boyfriend, whatever. My point is that many times, when men flirt with women and get rejected, they think they are losers and never do it again. *NOT TRUE*! It is a numbers game!

In sales, the odds are that if you call on one hundred people you may get ten interested in your product (the product being *YOU*) and out of that ten only two people will be interested in buying. If you are only talking with one person a week the odds are definitely not in your favor. Increase those odds daily by *"FLIRTING WITH LIFE"* ™ and talking to at least a few new people daily to get more practice and get comfortable talking to people. You will have more fun along the way as you connect with a stranger who might become your next girlfriend, best friend or at least may know someone that you might like!

Each day, take at least two risks that you wouldn't ordinarily take. This is how you grow. Many men are really "chicken" and they have to be introduced to a woman or sit next to her in a class for thirty sessions before speaking to her! Remember most people go through that three-to-four minutes of awkwardness when first connecting. It is scary for everyone, but the more risks you take, the easier it becomes. There are some clear signs that a women is not interested. Become alert to these signals to know if there is a red light and you are wasting your time.

Clear "Red Light" Signals
A Woman Who is <u>Not</u> Interested Will:

- *Close off her body language by crossing her arms and/or legs*
- *Say things like: " No thank-you, I have a boyfriend.", "I'm here with my friends and I can't talk right now.", "Nice to meet you. I'll talk to you later" or "I'm going to go circulate with my friends now."*
- *Be looking at everyone else but you*
- *Cut off all eye contact*
- *Turn her body away from you. If you get a shoulder you may be receiving the "cold" shoulder*
- *Back up and distance herself*
- *Change her energy suddenly to disinterest towards you and focus back to a friend she is with*
- *Put the focus on an activity happening in the room to change the subject*
- *Ignore your questions and pretend she didn't hear you so she doesn't have to feel awkward*
- *Give answers that are quick and short*
- *Become suddenly disinterested or sometimes cold if you answered a question that didn't mix with her values (religious affiliation, age she is comfortable dating, family values, where you live, occupation, recent breakup...)*

If you meet a woman that likes you and you don't feel a connection, just practice the art of flirting with her in the moment. Be kind and have compassion. You know how rejection feels. No lies — just be a gentleman, and remember she has the "rejection monster" voice in her head just the same as you. Since you are not that worried now about closing the deal with her, you will be able to relax and have fun. When you are kind to a woman, other women are watching you and can sense if you are considerate or not. Then when you go for the woman to whom you are more attracted later, she may feel safer to talk with you because you have an open, kind energy. You could be going after a woman that looks like a playboy bunny, but if she isn't into you or is a bitch, who cares, it doesn't matter how pretty she is. Find someone who turns you on energetically — and all the while, make friends with women that are into you, because they may just introduce you to someone that could be "the one."

Remember, flirting is easy if you do it with people all day. The word "flirting" means *"one who plays with courtship; a sudden throw; give a brisk motion to."* Flirting is energy sent toward a person who interests you. Flirting isn't always about attracting a romantic relationship, but for a joyful moment in time. When you connect with strangers daily, you can practice asking questions, you can work on actively listening, and you'll learn to read the vibrations and energy of people. You may want to be extra thoughtful to a stranger, compliment someone you would not normally look at, or surprise a person by smiling and saying *"Hello."* Be a person that is open to energy! I bet you will stay away from those angry, scowling people now that you are aware of energy vibes.

When you start flirting with women — even saying hello to anyone — may seem awkward at first. That's why you will practice *FLIRTING WITH LIFE!* ™ for a while to get used to the new way of being in the world. Then it becomes easier when you begin approaching women you desire. It will be more natural, because you do it all the time with other humans. You will make the attempt to overcome your shyness and your fears; you can create a new life! Here's the *SUCCESS FORMULA* to get you moving in the right direction!

S-U-C-C-E-S-S F-O-R-M-U-L-A
FOR MEETING NEW PEOPLE

SENSES - Your gut feelings are usually correct. Use your senses to feel out situations and energy. Your intentions should be sincere, or you could turn people off. Practice being more in-tune with your feelings by slowing down for a minute and taking a few, deep breaths and get in touch with all your senses.

UNIQUENESS - Be unique with the props that will make you stand out in a group. Wear a "Save the Dolphins" button, carry a colorful backpack, wear unusual ties, watches and sunglasses. Approach each person by noticing what is unique or special about him or her. Observe what is attractive to you and acknowledge it. We all love to be acknowledged.

CONSCIOUSNESS - Remain conscious of your energy and the words you use when flirting. These are your most powerful tools for making connections.

CONNECTION - Make connections by looking at people and listening with wonderment in your eyes. Be curious and ask questions that elicit more than a "yes" or "no" answer. Really connect for longer than a glance. This is difficult for some people to do, but it can open doors to deeper connecting if you go first! When you look into someone's eyes, you can connect deeper, and they feel it. The connection is either there or it's not.

ENERGY - Project the energy you wish to attract! Put yourself in a higher energy vibe with deep breathing (10 deep breaths before a meeting, party, or any social situation, especially when you feel tired or nervous). Talk to yourself about having a great time and only meeting interesting and amazing people! Workout, if you can, before going out. Take a brisk walk. Listen to inspiring music that makes you feel like dancing. Follow the energy tools in the previous chapter.

SUCCESS THINKING - Think, act, and respond like a winner, and you will win. Remember that flirting is a numbers game, and eventually you will connect. Think success and use your consciousness to create the feeling of success before going out!

SENSITIVITY - Be sensitive to other people and their vibes. Listen to the signs and use your senses to detect open or closed people.

FACIAL EXPRESSIONS - Facial expressions are a key to send the right signals. SMILE! Be open. Flirt with your eyes and expressions. If you can't look a woman in the eye directly, look at her mouth, and it will appear that you are looking directly at her eyes (a top-secret tip for the shy flirter). Try it. . . it works!

ORIGINALITY - Be an original. This goes for the way you dress to the topics you speak about. Read the paper and interesting books that add to your conversations. Use lines that fit your unique style and be sincere in the delivery. People can sense a phony.

RISK - Be brave! Talk to those people who interest you, and if you get a feeling of rejection, RISK again with someone else. There are millions of people to meet! Use your rapport building skills and risk again!

MOVE ON - When the vibe isn't right, get the message and move on. Why waste your time trying to get someone interested when they aren't? Be real with yourself and get the hint. It is a drain to your energy and theirs to have them harshly reject you because you're not taking the hint. MOVE ON and keep going!!!

UNDIVIDED ATTENTION - Give people your undivided attention, even if you are not 100% interested. Women are always watching to see how you interact with others. We all appreciate it when people really give us their attention. We can feel it. Nod in response to the conversation; add your genuine comments to let the person know you've really heard them and have given them your full attention. People will always remember you.

LISTEN & LEARN - When you are attending an event, you need to keep your ears open in order to hear where you can make an entry into a conversation. Lean in as you speak. As you become more aware of other people's space, you will read how close you can lean in to them (and make sure you have clean breath).

ACT - Act as if I'm already your friend. It makes me feel that I've known you forever. Then, perhaps, I will want to know you forever!!!

> *"Be brave! Even if you're not, pretend to be.*
> *No one can tell the difference.*
> —**Life's Little Instruction Book**

WINNING OPENING LINES

Before approaching someone, take a deep breath (or a bunch of deep breaths), relax your body, and say things that are sincere and true for you. Stand up tall, smile, *LISTEN TO THEIR UNIQUE COMMUNICATION STYLE* and *BUILD RAPPORT!* Change the following "lines" to fit your personality and style. *PRACTICE, CONNECT, BE OPEN, and STAY UNATTACHED TO OUT-COMES.* Risk! Create! Have fun with it!

- *I have to tell you this: You're the first woman I've seen today who looks happy. It's so refreshing!! What is making you happy these days? I'd like the prescription.*
- *I'm a little shy, but I didn't want to miss this opportunity to meet you.*
- *I've been watching you dance — do you take lessons somewhere? You're an awesome dancer! Can we dance?*
- *I can tell you are an adventurous woman. What do you do in the world?*
- *Do you live in this area? I'm new around here and am searching for the best hair salon/ Italian food/ shoe repair/whatever.*
- *Where did you get that great smile? It made my day!*
- *Hello, my name is_____ (your name, and sincerely ask) How are you doing?*
- *I couldn't help but notice you. May I ask your name and join you for a drink?*
- *You look familiar. Don't I know you from the gym/church/ networking event?*
- *I overheard you say you were into_____ How long have you been involved with that?*

- *Would you mind if I read a section of your paper? What do you think about _____ (current issue of the day)?*
- *Your dog has quite a personality or what an incredible dog. He has a beautiful coat on him! What breed is he/she?*
- This worked for me: I noticed a photo of a project someone had laid out on a counter at my printer. I asked the person printing it, *"That looks interesting — what is it? Is this your project? Tell me how it started?"* We are still good friends and may be working on a project together.
- *This place is so beautiful! Do you visit often?*
- *Susan??? Oh, I'm sorry, you look just like a friend I recently met. So, what is your name?*
- At a dance club: *Great shoes! Those shoes look stylish/sexy on you. Do they hurt your feet? Perhaps you'd like a foot rub after I dance with you?*
- In line at a takeout: *"Don't you love the mashed potatoes here? They are the best!"* If you're still chatting, ask if you can join her for a quick bite.
- *I love the suit you're wearing!! You must be a businesswoman. What business are you in?*
- *Is this something a woman would like as a gift? It's my sister's birthday, and I want to make sure she would enjoy this. What would your favorite gift be?*
- *We seem to be headed in the same direction. Would you like some company?*
- *(In the video store) Have you seen this film? Was Pacino as good as I've heard?*
- *I was watching you, and didn't want to let this opportunity to meet you pass me by ...My name is ...*
- *I saw you sitting alone — would you enjoy some company?*
- *That book you're reading. . . how is it? I've seen it everywhere. Where did you see it in here (if you're in a bookstore)?*
- *Would you mind helping me by spotting me on this exercise? This weight is heavy for me.*
- *I noticed you and I find you so attractive! How about having lunch/dinner/coffee ...or all three sometime?*
- *You obviously take very good care of yourself. You're in great shape. What do you do to maintain that muscle tone?*
- *I've never used (tried) this product before (at the perfume/*

cologne counter,7-11, takeout, the bakery, gourmet cooking store, the printer, the computer store, Radio Shack, hardware store, etc...) *do you know anything about it?*

♦ *Seeing you has made my day! I'd like to have the opportunity again soon.*

♦ *What would you like for dinner? I'm buying.*

♦ *You've got great energy! Where did you get it? How can I get some?*

♦ *I have seen you before, and I was intrigued by you. I would love to learn more about you. Can we go for coffee tomorrow?*

♦ *At a wedding: Are you a friend of the bride or the groom? Would you like to dance?*

♦ *Excuse me, didn't you go to _____ (the name of your high school/college/university)? Use this when they are wearing the sweatshirt from their university. They usually answer, and then I proceed with questions concerning the school, what they studied...???*

♦ *While rollerblading or skating, etc... stumble (gently!) into a person so they will stop, and then you can say something charming like: "I'm improving. . . sorry, but it was worth it to run into you! Want to give me some lessons?"*

♦ *After seeing you in _____ (red, blue, whatever color they're wearing), now I know that's going to become my favorite color.*

♦ *I love what you're wearing. How about if you wear that when I take you out to dinner?*

♦ *Do you happen to know where they keep the _____ (language tapes, art supplies, literature books, flour, olive oil, etc.)?*

♦ *You are a beautiful woman, and I want to know who you are/ My name is...*

A lot of guys believe that they have to come up with some clever or witty line in order to approach a woman. Unless you are a professional comedian or a natural wit, go easy on the jokes, or you may fall flat. If you happen to think of something funny or clever, by all means, say it! Women love sincerity, wit, and genu-ineness. So, resist the impulse to use what you think are "cutesy" or "clever" lines, because they usually do not work. There's noth-ing more embarrassing than a guy who launches into an "act" or "routine" that doesn't match the energy of the moment.

The important thing is that you say something pleasant and authentic to a woman you find yourself attracted to when you're out and about. Guys initiate relationships, and most women are wait-ing for you to speak first! We love to be approached, if we are interested. Use your intuition and read the clear signs women send.

WHERE TO MAKE THE CONNECTION

It's normal for women to be approached in ordinary settings. Furthermore, women welcome it. It is flattering to be told you look nice or hear a compliment as long as it is genuine. It's common for a woman to be approached one to three times per day as she goes about her ordinary tasks. Women dress attractively or provoca-tively to feel confident, and many claim that they enjoy being ap-proached. If they aren't interested, you will know by their body language and response to you. Don't take it personally if you don't get a response right away. Use every opportunity as practice.

Let's run through a practice session that could hypothetically take place at a bookstore. You see an attractive woman. . . she's looking at a book, and she looks up and smiles at you. . . Walk over slowly. Do not move too quickly — that can scare a person. You don't want to invade her space; you want to create a safe situation and body distance so she has time to warm up to your approach. After a minute or two, you could say, *"Wow! I've never seen so many different books on* _____ *(* topics such as cooking, art...*) in my life! Do you recommend a particular book in this section? I'm learning to* _____ *(*cook, understand ancient history or what-ever section of the store you might be exploring*)."* Keep all of your comments positive and upbeat, i.e., *" This a great store? Is this your neighborhood?"* or *"Have you attended any interesting book signing events here?"* By asking her about herself, she will know you are interested, and if she is still talking to you after three or four minutes, you can be assured that she is open to your connection (as a friend, at least). There is an opportunity for you to say something about yourself, i.e., *"I love this area, because I am able to rollerblade and play volleyball year round when I'm off work. What do you do for fun?"* or *"Do you ever rollerblade or play volleyball? By the way, what is your name, neighbor?"*

If the woman is still standing there, you're in a good situation to ask her to get together. *"I've really enjoyed talking with you (use her name). Would you like to get a cup of coffee with me across the street?"* OR *"You said you like rollerblading — would you like to go rollerblading with me next Saturday?"* Now is a perfect time to say, *"I'd like to call you."* Not all women give out their phone numbers, but most will take your phone number, and sometimes they do call back. Be a "man with a plan" that comes from listening closely to the communication style and asking her to do something that fits with that style. Ask her to go to a specific place at a certain time.

Don't take *"No"* as personal rejection. Sure, it can be painful, and it is also a learning experience. Dale Carnegie says, *"The successful man will profit from his mistakes and try again in a different way!"* Also know, just because she responded to your good vibes doesn't mean she wants to date you. You can still feel fantastic about yourself even when you hear "No." Remember, the more "No's" you get, the closer you are to a "Yes."

Many guys are cowards when it comes to talking to women! Even successful, rich, handsome men can be overwhelmed and unable to push through those first three minutes of awkwardness to even get "up to bat." The more you work at meeting people, the better at it you will become. The idea is to be able to meet a stranger without a formal introduction. It can easily be done, especially if you go to one or two new places each week and are *"FLIRTING WITH LIFE."*™ Stay unattached to the outcome, have fun and you will have no pain. You can be traveling abroad and meet someone new and build a new life. It can happen anywhere at anytime!

BEST PLACES TO MEET SINGLE WOMEN:

YOGA CLASSES — You may not like yoga or exercise, but this is where you will find a lot of women. Yoga classes, in particular, are usually about 80% women. And, the women who attend yoga classes are usually centered, in tune, and in shape. Stay calm, because you will be surrounded with the regulars, and if you come off calm and centered and don't stare or gawk, women will chat with you after they get used to your presence. Sometimes it takes awhile, and you will know if a woman is interested when she says "*Hello*" a few times and hangs around. The other great news is you'll get in better shape.

CHAMBER OF COMMERCE NETWORKING EVENTS — If you're a businessman, go to a local chapter meeting often. They take place in different parts of town at least once a month. A lot of women I know who attend the Chamber of Commerce meetings are looking for men, and it is a great place to find out about other networking groups and events in your area. Each member gets a name tag and the whole event is centered around meeting people for business. Chamber meetings are a great place to practice your new flirting techniques. The cost is normally $15 and includes wine and food.

YOUR LOCAL MARKET, OUTDOOR MARKETS, GARAGE SALES — Look in your local newspaper — they are everywhere! More women attend than men. If you have a good spot, hold your own garage sale to get rid of your old things and meet your neighbors.

GYMS — Many think gyms are not a good place to meet people. I disagree. I've met a few of the men I ended up dating at the gym. If you are bored with your gym, get free passes and try new locations! Go to classes regularly to become familiar with the people in class and be open and send out friendly vibes, not horn-dog vibes.

BOOKSTORES — Attend lectures, poetry readings. . . sit and have coffee, listen to the music at their coffee shops. More women normally attend than men, unless it is related to investments, sports or the Internet.

INTERNET CLASSES/CONVENTIONS — There are free Internet classes in cafes and libraries composed of mostly singles having a great time meeting new people. Extended Education classes offer these all year long, as well as The LEARNING ANNEX, in New York, San Francisco and San Diego. There are also Internet seminars and conventions happening in your area to get people interested in the E-commerce-based businesses. A lot of entrepreneurs attend these seminars and you'll expand your mind.

ART AND CERAMICS CLASSES (LOCAL COLLEGES) — My gorgeous friend Herb teaches art and ceramics classes. He says, *"If men were smart, they'd take ceramics classes, because attendees are about 95% women."* If you're interested in learning to be an artist, check out your local college for art, painting, or sculpting classes. Sculpting is creative and fun because you're using your hands and your imagination.

POLITICAL CAMPAIGNS — Especially during Presidential elections, there are hundreds of places to volunteer in every city. This is a great place to see people repeatedly, to develop friendships and establish yourself within a community. Who knows what other opportunities might develop.

LANGUAGE CLUBS AND CLASSES — These are especially great to participate in before you go on a trip to another country — you may even meet someone who will be there at the same time.

CHURCHES — There are so many wonderful churches, and if you're not into organized religion, go to a transdenominational church (meaning it is open to anyone of any religious belief, i.e., Catholic, Jewish, Christian, Buddhist, and Hindu, etc.). I'd like to make it clear that I'm not advocating any particular religion. Just know that most churches have social activities and build community. Be open to try new experiences.

MASSAGE CLASSES — Not only can you receive massages, you can meet other people while learning an invaluable skill. You will be receiving massages and be practicing your massage techniques on others. This will open up your sensuality. Any woman will tell you; a man who can rub your head & feet is invaluable!

EXTENDED EDUCATION CLASSES, SUCH AS THE LEARNING ANNEX (Los Angeles, California, New York, San Francisco, San Diego) — These are often one time night classes (some are all day to weekly) with special topics of interest: painting, photography, business, stocks, starting your own health spa/meditation center. Look in your local paper for evening classes to make you a more interesting person, and while you're at it, learn what topics women are into. Classes on furniture painting, cooking, sensuality....

VIDEO STORES — Ask for an opinion of a film while exploring your options.

GROCERY STORES — Ask questions about products of fellow shoppers. Discuss the crowded store, notice a person's eating habits and make comments that are funny: "Looks like it's an ice cream party for you tonight (use the items in their cart for comment).

POST OFFICE — Go to a busy post office when you have some extra time. Be friendly and make someone's day with a compliment.

YOGURT SHOPS — Get a sample. Ask the beautiful woman standing in line if she has ever tried it and was it tasty? Offer to buy her one if it's going well.

SPORTING LEAGUES (VOLLEYBALL, SOFTBALL, BASKETBALL, TENNIS, RACQUETBALL, ETC.) — There are hundreds of leagues that are coed. If you're into sports, these are excellent places to meet singles. There are also golf clubs and hiking clubs — see your local newspaper.

MARATHONS, AND SPORTING EVENTS — Many events are fund raisers and are attended by all types of nice people committed to supporting community projects.

PROFESSIONAL MATCHMAKERS— There are many matchmaking companies that have successfully matched many people, especially you busy men who don't have time to meet women.

FLOWER SHOPS — Women love flowers, and they are being sold everywhere now. Buy a flower for a woman just to surprise her, and she will talk about you for weeks — or fall in love with you forever. Buy them for a friend or even a stranger. This happened to me outside of a 7-Eleven. I was buying a big bundle of flowers for my TV show that day, and I was kind to a man by helping him pick out his flowers. He bought mine for me before I had a chance to pay the attendant. I told the story on my show and have never forgotten it. I kissed him in the parking lot and gave him a big hug. Those flowers made my week, as they would do for most women. If men only knew how happy flowers make us! Every time we look at them we think of how romantic and thoughtful you are.

DANCE CLASSES/CLUBS — Clubs sometimes offer free classes, i.e., two-step, and salsa (from 6pm-9pm). Women who love to dance are filled with energy — they are fun and usually in great shape! Even better, women love men who know how to dance. When you're up there moving on the dance floor, women are looking at you to see what you'll be like in bed! I'll give you an example: *"Did you have a date last night?"* *"Yeah. I went out with this cute guy, but he was a dud dancer. Forget him."* *"What do you mean? You didn't even give him a chance."* *"He couldn't even move his hips — he'd more than likely be lousy in bed."* That's what women say. You've got to learn to move your body, because if you can't move on the dance floor, you probably can't move it anywhere else either. I'm not trying to be hard on you guys — it's just the plain truth!

PARTIES (THROUGH FRIENDS AND SINGLES GROUPS) — This is one of the #1 places to meet, because other people can introduce you around or you can directly ask women attending how they got invited. Offer to become the party photographer and easily meet everyone! Offer to help the host set up! She will be talking to her friends about you all night!

WEDDINGS — The bride, no doubt, has fifteen girlfriends who are going to be there asking, *"Will there be any single men coming to the wedding?"* Men usually say, *"I don't want to go alone to a wedding. It will be boring."* As a result, there are usually a lot more women. You are missing out. More people I know have met at weddings than any other event. Everyone attending is in the mood to celebrate and open to meeting friends of the family. They are all dressed up and feeling good! This is an opportunity to connect by conversing about the bride-and-groom.

ART GALLERIES — Look in your local newspapers for openings/cocktail parties/exhibits. They are always interesting and a great and easy place to flirt. Use the art to create conversation. There are normally more women than men.

SHOPPING MALLS — In case you haven't already discovered it, women love to shop, especially at lovely malls. Many men I know meet a lot of women by shopping at exclusive boutiques claiming to be looking for a gift for their sister. One friend will buy a gift and have the girl wrap it, all the while finding out about her. If the salesclerk was taken by his charm and desire to be thoughtful, even if he's not right for her, she will introduce him to other women.

BOXING/TAE BO ™ **CLASSES**— A great way to get up-close and personal with new people and get in shape. Wear deodorant.

WALKING YOUR DOG — If you don't have a dog, you can always borrow one! Dogs are a great way to meet people. Cute dogs! Take your neighbor's dog for a walk in the evening and stop by the local coffee shop. Women love dogs, and many times dogs are magnets!

AT A RED LIGHT — **SMILE!** — Some of the friends I know are great at meeting new people at red lights — they'll roll down their window and shout, "Hey, you wanna have coffee sometime?"

VOLUNTEER AT YOUR LOCAL PUBLIC ACCESS TELEVISION STATION — I have met so many wonderful people at the local public access television station. If you have spare time and are interested in "the business" and you want to meet people involved in production, volunteer for two hours once or twice a month and learn how to operate cameras and meet a lot of new people.

CAFES AND RESTAURANTS — Check your local papers and explore Strike up a conversation with a stranger!.

the latest restaurants so you will have interesting places to take your dates later on. Flirt and then send over a drink or dessert. Strike up casual conversations.

CAR WASHES — On Saturdays, a lot of women take their cars to get washed, and while waiting, you'll have 5-10 minutes to strike up a conversation.

LAUNDRY ROOM, LAUNDROMATS AND DRY CLEANERS — Casual conversations. *"What's the best way to keep bright-colored clothes from fading?"* You'll have to be quick at the dry cleaner!

COSMETICS COUNTERS AT DEPARTMENT STORES — *"Do you know what SPF I would need for my type of skin?"*

OFFICE BUILDINGS AND CAFETERIAS — If you know everyone in your building, go to the building next door and have lunch in the cafeteria, or go to restaurants in the area. You may notice a particular woman on more than one occasion — many people frequent certain restaurants for lunch that are close to their office. Make a mental note, and on the following week go back on the same day at the same time.

AT THE BEACH, SUNBATHING — *"How did you get so tanned?"* *"What suntan lotion are you using?"* *"Do you need some on your back."*

LIBRARIES — The copy machines are great places to chat. *"How long are you going to be?"* then while you're waiting, strike up a conversation. Act lost and ask questions.

HAIR SALONS/NAIL SALONS (FOR A MANICURE) — As mentioned earlier, hairstylists and manicurists are notorious matchmakers. Go to an active salon that has class and style. Go where the women go and just get a trim so you can come back more often.

COMMUNITY THEATRE/ACTING /IMPROV CLASSES — These classes and theatres are great places to express yourself and connect with people from all walks of life. You get to live out some of your fantasies on stage!

TRADE SHOWS/CRAFT SHOWS — You will meet people from all walks of life who are into a particular field, e.g., computers, decorat-

shows, antique shows, retail product shows, health and fitness shows. Bring your business cards.

MUSIC STORES — With so many stores providing a place to hear the music first, you can be in a store for a while listing to all the different new releases. It's a great conversation starter. "Excuse me. Do you happen to know what the name of _____'s (your favorite artist here) new album is?

TRAVELING — Wilderness adventure clubs, bicycle clubs, ski clubs, singles tours, Club Med, traveling singles clubs and world wide cruises.

CHARITIES AND ORGANIZATIONS — When we do service work and volunteer, our compassionate side comes out. Many singles volunteer, and if you do it with an open heart and mind, you will meet new friends and possibly a new mate. Be open! The following is a list of charities that have chapters nationwide: Concern, Big Brothers, Share, Leukemia Foundation, D.A.R.E., Make a Wish Foundation, Starlight Foundation, Special Olympics, and many more — check on the web for volunteering in your local community. Giving your love while volunteering allows for people to see another part of your nature. Teach a class on your favorite subject in a childrens home, be a coach for special athletes, sing in an old age home, or feed the homeless. Start your own group and lead others to a cause you are passionate about. By giving back, you will be sending out the vibration of love, and receive gifts you have only dreamed of. The inspiration I have received from these organizations has been one of the driving forces of my company. Get involved!

ONLINE DATING — Connect with the world! Use your new knowledge and creative communication skills to meet interesting people on the internet! After reviewing what you are looking for in a mate, you can use the descriptive adjectives (in chapter 5) to write your ad. Many personal services, tele-chat and online dating services are reasonable or have trial times that are free! If you are open, you can meet great people — it's a numbers game. I have three close friends who married the men they met through personal ads, and I know hundreds who have met online. Make sure you have a good photo taken to use online. A picture can make a world of difference and most women won't answer an ad without one! Use your new communication skills to write powerful ads that magnetize people towards you! This medium for meeting is the latest and greatest way to connect. Get creative...buy a webcam! Soon we will all be talking live!

Utilizing all your new learned skills of energy and communicating clearly about what you want will make your online dating experience a lot more successful and enjoyable. In real life it is a numbers game, and the fact that online dating increases your odds is a motivation to keep you open to finding the mate of your dreams. Some people expect results overnight and others get disappointed by people lying about who they are. It happens. Online connecting is just another chance to expand your social circle. Give it a try!

Whenever you are out connecting, realize that people love to talk about themselves. To become a good conversationalist, you must ask questions that will require more than a "yes" or "no" answer. After listening to someone talk or when participating in a group conversation, you can pick up questions to ask that will continue the connection. Wherever you are, look and listen for connecting points to use as icebreakers and *PRACTICE!*

Use those great questions (in chapter 3) when meeting others, and you will have interesting conversations. I promise.

Now let's discover how to become a "Man with a Plan"...

YOU'RE IN THE DRIVER'S SEAT

Destiny is not a matter of chance, it is a matter of choice: it is not a thing to be waited for, it is a thing to be achieved.

William Jennings Bryan

BECOME A "MAN WITH A PLAN"

Now you're in the driver seat! When you call a woman, be a *"Man with a Plan"* and you're more likely to get her to go out with you. Women love a creative man who comes up with interesting, fun dates. If you've been dating someone for awhile, keep it interesting by being adventurous and varying the things you do together.

Call her with a plan in mind. *"I'd love to take you to a great theater production next Friday night. We'll get all dressed up and have dinner beforehand. What do you say?"* or *"I'm planning a day ski trip and couldn't think of anyone I'd rather take — are you available Saturday?"* This makes women feel so special! It's romantic! It feels soooo good when a man takes the lead. We feel cherished.

Plan ahead and clean out your car. Have gas in it and get it washed regularly. Yes, women do notice your car, and if it's clean, that makes up for the make and model. Have some good tunes to listen to and breath mints on you or in your glove box. Some men I know keep cologne in their car or they have their tune-up kit for emergency cleanups. Be prepared for those spur-of-the-moment plans. Call if your running late and let her know what you might be wearing if it is a special evening! Most importantly, be creative, and don't be cheap! If you're on a budget, many of these dates are reasonably priced.

GREAT DATES

- *Concerts — In your local paper, check for free concerts and events at the local universities. In Southern California, you can go from the Greek Theatre to the Forum to free concerts on the pier, Century City, and other locations.*
- *Day trip to other little towns nearby-- Every weekend there are art exhibits (great shops, restaurants).*
- *Hot springs. Check for massage and dinner specials. Bring sparkling champagne or cider with glasses.*
- *Food festivals. Greek, Italian, Garlic...check your local listings.*
- *Art exhibits all the time. Call all your local galleries and get on their mailing lists to receive invites ahead of time.*
- *Conventions. From cooking, to politics, to exotic animals, to gem shows, they are always educational and fun to explore.*
- *Romantic walks on the beach/at the lake/in the woods. Bring snacks or a picnic.*
- *Day trip for lunch (and/or dinner) to a restaurant with a view to remember. Bring a camera to make memories.*
- *Rent a boat for a night ride at a lake nearby, along the coast or go on a gondola ride. Extra bonus: hire a singer to serenade you.*
- *Plan a dinner cruise with all the bells and whistles. Call ahead to make sure they have the perfect table, and have flowers there before you arrive.*
- *Have dinner at one place, dessert at another, then switch again*

for the grand finale: after dinner drinks at a romantic club for dancing.

- Go to a great jazz club and share appetizers.
- Explore Chinatown, if you have one nearby.
- Go to a day spa and get pampered together.
- Go on a retreat together and learn meditation.
- Go out dancing to a place that has oldies or disco. Its great exercise!! (check listings for special nights).
- How about exercising together? Yoga, Boxing, aerobics. It gets those pheromones pumping and your muscles in shape.
- Take a seminar together. Learn massage, dancing, Internet.
- Go to a romance shop. Buy a toy or a game to play together.
- Go shoe/hat shopping. It's fun!, and you can find out a lot about a person.
- Have a massage party. . .Exchange scalp massages. Use relaxing aromatherapy. Give and receive. . .practice makes perfect!
- Beach or lake with a picnic and games. Don't forget the sunscreen or bug repellant.
- A drive to a local city. Check out the great art galleries and bistros nearby.
- Meet her for a rendezvous during work, and bring her lunch and flowers.
- Window shopping in your hottest shopping area. Stop and try on some great shoes or clothes and have a little fun in the fitting room.
- Plays/Theatre. Reasonable to expensive, sometimes, you can get rush tickets.
- Get a movie and dinner and bring it over. Especially on a low-key night.
- A romantic walk by a boat dock. Check out those yachts!!!
- A trip to the local planetarium to look at the stars.
- Go shoot a game of pool.
- Film Festivals. Lots of artsy and unique European films.
- Networking events. If it's something she is interested in.
- Holiday/Theme Parties. Invite her along to Halloween par-

ties, hat, toga or Super Bowl parties...or throw one of your own!

- Walk in the woods with a blanket and some romantic poetry to read to each other.
- Fairs and carnivals in your local community — win her a teddy bear.
- Interactive theatre. "Tony and Tina's Wedding", Murder Mystery train rides.
- Take her on a train ride with your own cabin and have dinner served.
- Go horseback riding at night in the mountains or on the beach, then stop for a snack.
- How about a foot massage party?
- Help her shop to update her wardrobe.
- Pack a snack and go for a stroll in the park.
- Rollerblading, biking, or a good run is always fun.
- A day ski trip.
- Home Depot and local hardware stores. Nothing like helping a woman repair a few things around the house!
- Go on a great hike or a day trip to the mountains. Bring snacks!!!
- Wine tasting parties, then go out for Italian food!
- Go on a gondola ride in Naples. Long Beach or Venice, Italy, of course.
- Stop by travel agencies and pick up brochures for some exotic vacations. Plan one!
- Go to one of those new ceramics places where you can paint your own piece of ceramics to take as a memory. It is so much fun to discover the talents you and your date have together.
- Go to a local pier and go on the rides or play pinball, video games, and have your pictures taken in a photo booth.
- When out on an ordinary date and she comments that she likes something in a window, go buy it for her on the spot. She will talk about that for weeks.
- Rent a Harley and helmets and pick her up for a ride in the hills.
- Go to a total entertainment center with the new virtual reality

games and speed raceway. Act like kids!
♦ *Bowling-in-the-dark at certain alleys! Bowling is fun anyway!*
♦ *Magic Shows.*
♦ *Meet for coffee or tea midday to steal a kiss!*
♦ *Go have your palms read together to see what is in store for you in the future.*
♦ *Go to see a TV show taping.*
♦ *Give her a bath. All the fixings: bubbles, candles, incense, and, of course, relaxing music — join her, then wash her hair!*
♦ *Go to a comedy club.*
♦ *Sing Karaoke and have a few laughs.*
♦ *Go to a drive-in movie and bring a blanket to snuggle under.*

Whatever you do...Be Spontaneous and Adventurous.

THE FINAL WORD

Now that you have these refining tools, it is up to you to incorporate these winning techniques into your daily life. This work will put you in the driver's seat and in control of your life's experiences. With the combination of the powerful inner and outer tune-ups, and by accepting your self for all of your strengths and idiosyncrasies, your life will reflect more balance and joy.

Be good to yourself and acknowledge the gifts you have to offer in a relationship. Communicate clearly about who you are and your desired outcome. You may choose to wait and take some time to get to know yourself before getting involved in a relationship, you can casually date, or you may commit to finding your life partner. Whatever the case, getting in tune with yourself and being honest about what phase you are in will assist you in your process. Remember, you have to *first* become the type of person you are looking for!

As you let go of expectations and are open to expanding and learning from all your connections, you never know where you might meet someone special. Remember, it's not quantity but quality you are after. You may have to play the numbers game for awhile, but it's only a matter of time before you meet that "*ONE*" special person. Smile more! Connect deeper! Become the loving person you are searching for! Keep "FLIRTING WITH LIFE"™ and enjoy the ride! You will experience new levels of passion and fulfillment in your life. Keep in touch and please contact me with your success stories and comments! I'd love to hear from you.

The preparation, courting and dating experiences are only the beginning of the journey. My next series of books will assist you with the other areas of love, sex, communication and many issues we haven't covered.

You're a man with a Winning Plan that will work, if you work it!

MORE INFORMATION ABOUT LOVE MECHANICS

If you would like to set up a **private coaching** session with Renee Piane by phone or in person, she can be reached at her office 310-442-9700 or 310-285-3636 or email at Coach@LoveMechanics.com.

Listen for Renee Piane on the **radio**. Check the web site at www.LoveMechanics.com for times and dates. If you have a product, service, seminar or special story and would like to be interviewed, please send an email to Radio@LoveMechanics.com.

Renee Piane is also available for **seminars,** book signings, radio and television interviews. Please send an email along with your request to Renee@LoveMechanics.com.

Please check our **web site** for our *Love Tune-Up Center* offering other great products carefully designed to enrich your life personally and professionally ... such as Renee's skin care line for men ... services and other networking events offered by Renee Piane through her web site www.LoveMechanics.com.

Please take a moment to share your thoughts and ideas through our **online survey** which will help contribute to many upcoming articles, book reviews, radio shows and future book topics ... Your opinions matter!

If you would like to share a personal **testimonial** or story about how *Love Mechanics* has positively effected your life or relationship, we would love to hear from you. Please email your testimony or story to us at MyStory@LoveMechanics.com or visit the web site at www.LoveMechanics.com to fill out our online testimonial form.

Remember ... **LOVE WORKS!** Pass it on!

To Order More Copies of Love Mechanics

Internet Orders: www.LoveMechanics.com
Telephone Orders: (310) 442-9700 or (310) 285-3636
Fax Orders: (310) 656-0027
Postal Orders: Love Mechanics
           c/o Love Works Publishing
           1453-A 14th Street, Suite 277
           Santa Monica, CA 90404

(For postal orders, mail this order form with your payment to the above address. Do not send cash and no CODs.)

Name:_____

Address:_____

City:_____

State:_____Zip:_____

Country:_____

Phone Number:_____

Email Address:_____

Credit Card Type:　　[　] Visa　　[　] Master Card

Credit Card Number:_____

Expiration Date:_____

Billing Address:_____

City:_____

State:_____Zip:_____

Country:_____

PRICE: $19.95 ea. plus $3.95 S&H

California Residents add applicable sales tax.

TOTAL $_____(add $3.00 for orders shipped outside U.S.)

Prices and availability subject to change without notice. Please allow four to six weeks for delivery. Thank you for your order!